T0306703

Developing Tailored Supply Strategies

Nancy Y. Moore, Clifford A. Grammich, Robert Bickel

Prepared for the United States Air Force
Approved for public release; distribution unlimited

RAND PROJECT AIR FORCE

The research described in this report was sponsored by the United States Air Force under Contracts F49642-01-C-0003 and FA7014-06-C-0001. Further information may be obtained from the Strategic Planning Division, Directorate of Plans, Hq USAF.

Library of Congress Cataloging-in-Publication Data

Moore, Nancy Y., 1947-
Developing tailored supply strategies / Nancy Y. Moore, Clifford A. Grammich, Robert Bickel.
p. cm.
Includes bibliographical references.
ISBN 978-0-8330-4120-3 (pbk. : alk. paper)
1. United States. Air Force—Procurement. 2. United States. Dept. of Defense—Procurement. 3. Purchasing. 4. Industrial procurement—United States. 5. Business logistics—United States. I. Grammich, Clifford A. (Clifford Anthony), 1963– II. Bickel, Robert W. III. Title.

UG1123.M66 2007
355.6'21—dc22

2007023211

The RAND Corporation is a nonprofit research organization providing objective analysis and effective solutions that address the challenges facing the public and private sectors around the world. RAND's publications do not necessarily reflect the opinions of its research clients and sponsors.

RAND® is a registered trademark.

© Copyright 2007 RAND Corporation

All rights reserved. No part of this book may be reproduced in any form by any electronic or mechanical means (including photocopying, recording, or information storage and retrieval) without permission in writing from RAND.

Published 2007 by the RAND Corporation
1776 Main Street, P.O. Box 2138, Santa Monica, CA 90407-2138
1200 South Hayes Street, Arlington, VA 22202-5050
4570 Fifth Avenue, Suite 600, Pittsburgh, PA 15213-2665
RAND URL: http://www.rand.org/
To order RAND documents or to obtain additional information, contact
Distribution Services: Telephone: (310) 451-7002;
Fax: (310) 451-6915; Email: order@rand.org

Preface

Best commercial sourcing practice recommends the development of supply strategies for all key goods and services prior to actual procurement. This monograph is intended as a reference resource for the procurement and related functional personnel and managers who are responsible for developing supply strategies.

Our purpose here was not to analyze current procurement practices in the Air Force or the Department of Defense but rather to synthesize the business and professional literature on

- processes for targeting sourcing initiatives and developing methodologies for segmenting spend, suppliers, and supply relationships
- processes for developing enterprisewide sourcing strategies.

As a result, the process presented here for selecting supply initiatives and developing supply strategies is a composite of nearly a dozen different supply strategy processes found in the literature.

The material presented here should be of interest to managers seeking to improve their sourcing and supply management activities. It should help them better understand the organizational processes, activities, structures, and analytic skills needed to develop supply strategies and hence to support the implementation of best purchasing and supply management practices. It should be of interest to those who wish to learn more about developing supply strategies, particularly representatives of procurement, supply, and supply chain management for the Department of Defense or other large organizations.

This work was part of the overall analytical support for a RAND Project AIR FORCE study begun in fiscal year 2002, entitled "Designing, Implementing, and Evaluating a Purchasing and Supply Management (PSM) Demonstration for Engines." The research was sponsored by the Air Force Supply Chain Integration and Logistics Transformation Office (AF/IL-I) and the Air Force Deputy Assistant Secretary for Contracting (SAF/AQC). Appendix B leverages unpublished RAND Corporation research on purchasing and supply management for the Army. The material in this monograph on supply strategy segmentation has also been adapted to support changes in purchasing and supply management practices in the U.S. Army Materiel Command.

Research on this topic and related purchasing and supply chain management issues continues in the Resource Management Program of RAND Project AIR FORCE. Other RAND publications on PSM and spend analysis include

- *Implementing Best Purchasing and Supply Management Practices: Lessons from Innovative Commercial Firms*, by Nancy Y. Moore, Laura H. Baldwin, Frank Camm, and Cynthia R. Cook (DB-334-AF), 2002. Online at http://www.rand.org/pubs/documented_briefings/DB334/
- *Using a Spend Analysis to Help Identify Prospective Air Force Purchasing and Supply Management Initiatives*, by Nancy Y. Moore, Cynthia R. Cook, Clifford Grammich, and Charles Lindenblatt (DB-434-AF), 2004. Online at http://www.rand.org/pubs/documented_briefings/DB434/
- *Air Force Procurement Workforce Transformation: Lessons from the Commercial Sector*, by John Ausink, Laura H. Baldwin, and Christopher Paul (MG-214-AF), 2004. Online at http://www.rand.org/pubs/monographs/MG214/
- *Air Force Service Procurement: Approaches for Measurement and Management*, by Laura H. Baldwin, John A. Ausink, and Nancy Nicosia (MG-299-AF), 2005. Online at http://www.rand.org/pubs/monographs/MG299/
- *An Assessment of Air Force Data on Contract Expenditures*, by Lloyd Dixon, Chad Shirley, Laura H. Baldwin, John A. Ausink, and Nancy Campbell (MG-274-AF), 2005. Online at http://www.rand.org/pubs/monographs/MG274/

RAND Project AIR FORCE

RAND Project AIR FORCE (PAF), a division of the RAND Corporation, is the U.S. Air Force's federally funded research and development center for studies and analyses. PAF provides the Air Force with independent analyses of policy alternatives affecting the development, employment, combat readiness, and support of current and future aerospace forces. Research is conducted in four programs: Aerospace Force Development; Manpower, Personnel, and Training; Resource Management; and Strategy and Doctrine.

Additional information about PAF is available on our Web site at http://www.rand.org/paf/

Contents

Figures

Tables

Summary

Purchased goods and services are an increasingly large proportion of public and private enterprise budgets. Historically, purchased goods and services have accounted for less than a third of an enterprise's budget, but today many enterprises spend more than two-thirds of their budgets on purchased goods and services. Similarly, the Air Force and the Department of Defense (DoD) spend nearly half their budgets for purchased goods and services and an additional sixth on weapon procurement (with only a third going to military and civilian personnel costs). (See pp. 1–6.)

Because of the growing importance of purchasing, many enterprises have sought to develop supply strategies for their purchased goods and services. This monograph is intended as a resource for procurement personnel developing supply strategies for the Air Force or DoD. It does not analyze current military procurement practices but rather synthesizes academic, business, and professional literature on developing and applying supply strategies. Its core is a synthesis of nearly a dozen different processes found in the literature.

Supply Strategies and the Need to Tailor Them

A *supply strategy* is a proactive plan for acquiring and managing a group of goods or services. It outlines how the enterprise intends to ensure cost-effective, responsive, reliable, and high-quality supplies to meet current and future needs. It should be developed *before* there is a requirement. In contrast to traditional purchasing practices that *react* to a requirement, a supply strategy can support such tactics as

- aggregating similar or related requirements
- changing the number, composition, or workload of suppliers
- adjusting purchasing resource levels, capacities, or capabilities
- improving the inventory mix, size, or location
- changing other purchasing policies, practices, operations, or organizations in response to evolving organizational needs and marketplace conditions. (See pp. 6–9.)

For the Air Force, supply strategies should encompass the end-to-end value chain. That is, they should stretch "upstream" to the supply base, encompassing such goods and services as assemblies, subcomponents, and parts, as well as "downstream" to such products as weapon systems and, ultimately, to such customers as differing major commands. In many enterprises, purchasers may look only upstream, and logistics personnel may look only downstream, with both focusing on different objectives. Developing a supply strategy that minimizes total costs and maximizes value to customers requires looking both directions. (See pp. 9–13.)

Supply strategies should be tailored to varying characteristics of purchases, including the characteristics of the product, its importance and technology, supplier preferences and power, the strategic importance of the purchase, the buying power of the purchaser, and the cultures of the buyer and the supplier. For example, goods and services that have little strategic importance to an enterprise and for which little value can be added through supplier relationships will best be handled through efficient "arm's-length" relationships, while items having the greatest strategic importance and for which supplier relationships might be expected to add the greatest value should be acquired through more-sophisticated partnerships or strategic alliances. (See pp. 15–20.)

A Composite Supply Strategy Development Process

Several different processes and analytic frameworks in the academic, business, and professional literatures describe somewhat different ways to segment goods, services, and suppliers and to develop supply strategies. Many of the same or similar steps occur in more than one framework.

These processes have two primary phases. The first involves assessing and strategically targeting opportunities across an enterprise to improve supply processes and strategies by grouping, prioritizing, and providing resources for prospective supply strategy initiatives, while the second includes specific commodity initiatives tailored to particular needs and ideally selected for their ease of selection, the size and speed of their effects on business, and their ability to free up personnel (e.g., through automation of purchases) for other initiatives. (See pp. 21–22.)

Phase I: Assess, Group, Segment, and Prioritize Enterprisewide Opportunities

The first phase, opportunity assessment, documents current purchases and suppliers through an enterprisewide high-level spending analysis (or "spend" analysis) to determine the total amount the enterprise spends on goods and services and its expenditures by commodity, supplier, and other categories. The total buy identified by this analysis can then be segmented into major categories of direct spending (e.g., inputs to production processes) and indirect spending (e.g., information technology and telecommunications, overhead and support, facilities). Each category should be large enough to warrant significant resources and to help leverage economies of scale and scope. Relevant employees should be identified and involved in each part of the segmentation process.

The first phase of the supply-strategy development process, ultimately leading to identification and prioritizing of opportunities for applying strategic sourcing, consists of these steps:

- Assign an enterprisewide, cross-functional team to group, segment, and prioritize spending (determining enterprise expenditures by commodity and supplier).
- Document and analyze purchases and spending by category groups or subgroups.
- Document the current supply base and identify prospective risks.
- Segment and classify purchases by their strategic importance and other factors.
- Identify and quantify prospective opportunities.
- Assess capabilities and the ease of internal and external execution.
- Prioritize opportunities by expected benefit and effort.

The following subsections describe each in turn.

Assign an Enterprisewide, Cross-Functional Team to Group, Segment, and Prioritize Spending. The first step toward a supply strategy is establishing an enterprisewide cross-functional team to conduct or oversee analyses of spending, markets, industries, and suppliers and to develop and validate category groups or subgroups for segmenting and prioritizing spending.[1] Team members may represent such functions as purchasing, engineering, manufacturing, customer relations, supplier relations, logistics, quality control, and legal affairs. In particular, the team should include personnel from key functional areas who can provide many broad perspectives on each commodity, its end product, and its reasons for market success, as well as those who can provide funds and staffing for implementing selected strategies. (See pp. 22–23.)

Document and Analyze Purchases and Spending by Category Groups or Subgroups. Once in place, the team should begin by conducting or leading a spending analysis, evaluating spending categories by dollar value, number and type of contracts, contract terms, purchasing organizations, and frequency of purchase. A spending analysis should begin with an enterprisewide extraction of spending data from all available internal and external systems. An effective spending analysis requires aggregation of all spending data into a single consolidated view of the enterprise's overall spending. If it is feasible to do so, analysts should categorize spending data at the item level, providing visibility and allowing comparisons of detailed attributes across commodities and suppliers, including supplier financial viability and stability. The data should also enable a view of what the entire enterprise, as well as each of its divisions, sites, and individual

---

[1] Appendix A describes a process for grouping or aggregating requirements for sourcing.

buyers, spends with each supplier and for each commodity for the entire enterprise and should allow comparison of price and such other attributes as inflation, contract compliance, and premium cost variance. (See pp. 23–24.)

If item-level data are not available, higher-level data can still be used to illustrate opportunities to leverage purchases and make the case to senior management for allocating resources to implement new purchasing, supply, and supply chain management practices and to create a new purchasing organization or significantly restructure the current one. Within the Air Force, for example, DD350 data, though not optimal for a spending analysis because they lack item-level data, provide information on 97 percent of all Air Force direct purchases in fiscal year 2005. (See pp. 24–25.)

Document the Current Supply Base and Identify Prospective Risks. To document the supply base and identify risks, the team should look at the enterprise's total number of suppliers, its total spend, the portfolio of products it purchases, and the related performance of its suppliers. The buyer should also evaluate the supplier base by industry, firm, geography, market risk (e.g., variations in supply availability, costs, and performance), and other relevant variables. Supplier data should also include geographical issues, dependency (the percentage of a supplier's business associated with a particular buyer and the percentage of a given commodity that a supplier provides that buyer), logistics costs, and other policy variables. In sum, a buyer should identify key indicators for prospective improvements in purchasing and supply management. (See pp. 25–26.)

Segment and Classify Purchases by Their Strategic Importance and Other Factors. Once purchases and the supply base have been documented, they should be categorized by value, volume, risks, and other variables that can affect the performance of an enterprise. Different commodities or buyer goals may dictate different categories. Commodity groups may have varying characteristics, dictating different supply strategies. Portfolio analysis may be used to classify commodities by their vulnerability (e.g., level of supply risk or strategic importance to the enterprise) and value (e.g., relative cost, influence on profits). The resulting segmentation can be used to place commodities in one of four groups:

- *Noncritical* goods and services have low vulnerability and low value (e.g., office supplies and furniture, standard hardware and electrical components, travel services).
- *Leverage* goods and services have high value but low vulnerability (e.g., basic production materials, standard information technology, logistics services).
- *Bottleneck* goods and services have low value but high vulnerability (e.g., unique or specifically engineered parts, capital equipment).
- *Strategic* goods and services have high value and high vulnerability (e.g., aircraft engines, specialized software, pharmaceuticals). (See pp. 26–41.)

Identify and Quantify Prospective Opportunities. Once commodities have been so categorized, buyers can seek to identify and quantify opportunities to improve operations of the enterprise. This can include working through corporate family relationships, interrelated suppliers, and duplicate suppliers while working within the requirements of special policies (e.g., federal mandates for procurement from small and disadvantaged businesses). Evaluating the expected rewards and risks includes identifying expected cost and performance improvements and the timing and required resources to obtain them. Efforts that require too many resources or too much time to produce results are unlikely to sustain interest and support from senior management, particularly for initial efforts. (See pp. 41–42.)

Suppliers with multiple contracts, multiple suppliers providing similar products or services, or different agencies purchasing the same goods or services all indicate prospective opportunities for savings through consolidation of purchases. Corporate family relationships, interrelated suppliers, and duplicate suppliers can likewise indicate possibilities for buyers to consolidate and leverage spending and to reduce transaction costs. Supplier cost growth exceeding that of the Producer Price Index may indicate that a supplier is not doing enough to control costs or to identify opportunities for savings. Supplier performance data demonstrating varied or poor quality, long or inconsistent wait times, little information sharing or supplier innovation, and few multiyear contracts may indicate opportunities for performance improvement. (See pp. 42–43.)

The opportunities an enterprise has to realize savings can vary according to its current spending and to broader market conditions. An enterprise will, for example, have greater potential for savings on a standard commodity for which it pays a great deal than on those for which it pays relatively little. Similarly, a highly fragmented supply base and modest contractual agreements indicate areas for improvement, while strong contractual agreements may indicate a supply base that has already been leveraged. A simple market with few suppliers or one at full capacity indicates limited potential for savings, while a complex competitive market indicates greater potential for savings. (See p. 43.)

Assess Capabilities and the Ease of Internal and External Execution. Enterprises are unlikely at first be able to pursue all prospective opportunities of savings through improvements in purchasing and supply strategies. The team must consider several variables related to the internal and external environments of the enterprise as they consider how to add value to purchasing processes. Internally, enterprise culture, personnel readiness and workload, competitive priorities, functional relationships, reward systems, data availability, and preexisting policy goals can affect the ability of an enterprise to pursue savings through more-innovative supply strategies. Such variables can affect the ability of an organization to gain visibility into its purchasing practices and implement strategies to improve them. Externally, the competition prevalent in the industry and the legal and political circumstances can also affect opportunities for realizing savings. Competitive factors influencing the ability of an enterprise to realize savings through supply strategies include its core competencies, the characteristics of its customers, the structure of its industry, the sources and levels of its competition, the capabilities of its supply base, the technology of the commodity, and any uncertainty in the market. (See pp. 43–45.)

The degree of effort needed for a successful supply strategy will also vary by enterprise and commodity. Among determinants of necessary effort are the complexity of the good or service, the potential for alternative suppliers, the level of centralization within the enterprise, current contractual obligations, and the ability of the enterprise to change suppliers. (See p. 46.)

Prioritize Opportunities by Expected Benefit and Effort. Once the prospective business effects of and the degree of effort needed to develop and execute a specific supply strategy for a commodity has been estimated, the team can prioritize opportunities for cost savings and performance improvements according to expected effectiveness and effort. One means of doing this is plotting each commodity group on a matrix similar to that used for supply segmentation, with axes representing business effectiveness and degree of effort required. The highest priority targets should be the commodity groups requiring the least effort but having the greatest value. Enterprises may also wish to prioritize initiatives for noncritical items with high numbers of transactions, perhaps automating these so as to free personnel to address other more critical goods and services. (See p. 45.)

Phase II: Develop Supply Strategies for the Commodity Group Initiatives with the Greatest Value and Fastest Payback

Segmenting and prioritizing the commodities prepares buyers to tailor and execute appropriate supply strategies for each, selecting these according to ease of execution and greatest likely benefit to the enterprise Many of the steps in this second phase parallel those in the first but with more-detailed, more-rigorous, in-depth analysis of specific commodities rather than the entire spending pattern of an enterprise (see pp. 50–51):

- Assign a cross-functional team to and provide resources for each commodity initiative.
- Develop a more-detailed profile of the selected commodity group.
- Analyze the industry and the supply market for the specific commodity group.
- Identify and prioritize prospective risks and vulnerabilities.
- Develop a strategy.
- Execute the strategy.

Assign a Cross-Functional Team to and Provide Resources for Each Commodity Initiative. As before, the first step is to establish an enterprisewide cross-functional team—or rather, in this case, one team for each of the most promising commodity groups identified in phase I. These cross-functional teams will be more specialized and more focused and will have deeper expertise in the commodity than the team in phase I. The members of each commodity team should have backgrounds and skills that focus more specifically on that commodity and who therefore are better able to analyze it more rigorously. Including members from various enterprise units (for a conglomerate like DoD) and functions in these teams will help ensure support across the enterprise for the supply strategies they develop and will lead to a more-rigorous examination of current requirements, the capabilities of the supply base, and a longer-term view of purchasing decisions.[2] (See pp. 50–51.)

Develop a More-Detailed Profile of the Selected Commodity Group. The team, once assembled, develops a more-detailed profile of its chosen commodity group. The profile will include user requirements and priorities, the demand, order quantities and patterns, spending, prices and total costs, specifications, the performance of the current supply base, and an initial assessment of opportunities for a supply strategy. (See pp. 51–52.)

Analyze the Industry and the Supply Market for the Specific Commodity Group. After developing a detailed profile of the specific good or service, the team should analyze the industry and the supply market for it. This analysis would include determining how the commodity fits into the value stream of the enterprise; determining supplier costs, capabilities, portfolios, and strategies; assessing the structure of the industry; and determining the relative power of the buyer and supplier. (See pp. 52–56.)

Industry and supply market analysis for a selected commodity group also recognizes that, just as buyers may segment their commodities and suppliers, suppliers may segment buyers and adopt strategies toward them. As suppliers may see it,

- *Nuisance* buyers may lack name recognition or a positive reputation and purchase goods and services of relatively low value. Suppliers are likely to show little interest or support for such customers.
- *Development* buyers have highly attractive businesses but relatively small profits. Suppliers may work hard at first to meet and exceed requirements of such customers in the hope of winning more of their business.
- *Exploitable* buyers have unfavorable operating conditions but purchase goods and services of relatively high value. Suppliers may seek maximum short-term benefit by raising prices.
- *Core* buyers purchase goods and services of high value and are thus highly attractive customers. Suppliers consider such customers to be the foundation of their business. (See pp. 56–57.)

---

[2] Appendix B discusses organizing for supply strategy development.

How buyers respond to supplier segmentation and strategies will depend on the structure of the supply industry and the nature and volume of related goods or services. Ideally, buyers would like to move from supplier to buyer dominance of the market and supply relationships. The ability to do so, however, is affected not only by the relative power of the buyer and the supplier but also by possibilities of substitution and the ability of new firms to enter the market. (See pp. 58–59.)

Identify and Prioritize Prospective Risks and Vulnerabilities. After analyzing the industry and the supply market for its commodity group, the commodity team identifies prospective risks and vulnerabilities throughout the value chain that could affect supply, determines the probability of these events, assesses their likely duration, and develops and prioritizes precautions for them. Events affecting supply may include natural disasters, fires, bombings and other terrorist attacks, and cartel actions or strikes that limit supply. (See pp. 59–60.)

Risks may vary by commodity, product, or service, and developing possible responses to them takes time and resources. Efforts to address supply risks are often therefore best focused first on the goods or services that are most strategic to the enterprise. That is, rather than seeking to address all vulnerable areas at once, commodity teams should focus on the precautions that are likely to bring the greatest relief to those most accountable for sales and profit performance. Commodity teams can initially focus on the events with the greatest likelihood of occurrence, that are likely to last the longest, and that would most affect the enterprise, particularly those involving strategic or bottleneck commodities with markets difficult to negotiate. (See pp. 60–63.)

Develop a Strategy. Once it has developed a rigorous commodity profile, analyzed the industry and supply market, and addressed the risks and vulnerabilities, the supply team can write a supply strategy. Supply strategies can vary by buying policy, number of sources, and types of sources. The strategies should define supplier roles, including areas for supplier integration and, in particular, should include buyer responses to supplier segmentation of noncritical, leverage, bottleneck, and strategic goods and services. Different categories of goods and services will require different buyer responses to otherwise similar supplier segmentations. Supply strategies should also set specific and measurable goals, which should extend beyond price to other variables affecting total cost, quality, and delivery, among others. Goals should be based on competitive analysis and comparison with marketplace leaders and be updated to reflect future marketplace trends. (See pp. 64–70.)

Execute the Strategy. Once the supply strategy has been developed and approved, the commodity team executes it. This involves identifying and prequalifying the best suppliers, issuing requests for proposals, selecting one or more suppliers, negotiating fact-based terms and conditions, finalizing the relationship and its metrics and incentives, managing the transition to any new suppliers, and monitoring the performance of both suppliers and the supply strategy. (See pp. 70–72.)

In considering supplier performance, buyers may wish to weigh the variables affecting supplier attractiveness and relationships against each other. If a supplier is attractive, perhaps offering a strategically important good or something difficult to purchase elsewhere, but if the supplier-buyer relationship is also not strong, a buyer might seek to improve the relationship by improving communication, providing the supplier with more volume, or involving it in product development. If the supplier-buyer relationship is relatively strong and if the supplier is also moderately or highly attractive, a buyer might wish to maintain that strong relationship but look for ways to manage it more effectively. If the supplier is not attractive, the buyer may wish to consider different suppliers, although it is also important to consider how the supplier influences its network position. (See pp. 72–73.)

The last component of execution is monitoring results and reviewing performance to determine whether the strategy is achieving its stated objectives or whether it requires modification. Key elements of monitoring and review include the following:

- meeting regularly to determine whether the strategy is well aligned with organizational objectives
- sharing results with top management to ensure that they continue to support the strategy and provide continuing momentum
- assessing internal customer and supplier perceptions
- determining whether key goals are being achieved
- executing contingency plans if accomplishments are lacking
- providing feedback to those involved, including lessons learned.

Supply strategies are iterative. Firms constantly revisit and reassess their decisions based on new information about demand and supply, supplier performance, customer needs, and other changes in market conditions. (See pp. 73–74.)

Conclusions

Leading enterprises are making significant commitments to changing their purchasing and supply management practices. They are analyzing their spending, segmenting it into major commodity groups based on their value to the enterprise and their vulnerability, and prioritizing them for initial purchasing and supply management efforts. The Air Force and DoD can use the same means to develop tailored supply strategies that should better support the warfighter. In fact, both the Air Force and DoD have already launched initiatives based on many of the best practices discussed here. (See pp. 75–76.)

Although some activities are common to most supply strategies, no one process is likely to fit all enterprises and commodities. An approach that delivers the most rewards to the enterprise will require extensive analysis.

Acknowledgments

The authors appreciate the support of and feedback from our Air Force project sponsors, Brig Gen (Ret.) Robert Mansfield, former Director of the Air Force Supply Chain Integration Logistics Transformation Office (AF/IL-I) in the office of the Deputy Chief of Staff for Installations and Logistics, and Grover Dunn, Director of Innovations and Transformation in the office of the Deputy Chief of Staff for Installations and Logistics, as well as our project officers for the study, Wing Commander Margaret Staib and Wing Commander Mark Leatham. We also appreciate the feedback we received on earlier versions of this document from Col (Ret.) Jeffrey Parsons, former Director of Contracting, Air Force Materiel Command (AFMC/PK); Roger (Scott) Correll, Director of Contracting, Ogden Air Logistics Center; George Faldane, formerly of the Warner-Robins Air Logistics Center Plans and Programs Directorate (WR-ALC/XP); and Lt Col David Reese, who, at the time of our study, was at the Coordination Center, Allied Command Component Headquarters, Ismir, Turkey, and now commands the 37th Contracting Squadron (Air Education and Training Command), Lackland Air Force Base, Texas.

Our RAND colleagues John Ausink, Laura Baldwin, and Frank Camm all reviewed several different earlier versions of this document. Camm also provided helpful input on an earlier version of our appendix on grouping requirements in supply strategy development. Ellen Pint of RAND and Lisa Ellram of Colorado State University also provided helpful reviews of the present version. We are also grateful for support of this research by Natalie Crawford, RAND Vice President and Director of RAND Project AIR FORCE, and C. Robert Roll, Director of the Project AIR FORCE Resource Management Program. We thank Carol Zaremba, Regina Sandberg, Terri Perkins, and Lacey Levitt for their work to prepare various versions of this manuscript for publication. Of course, all errors in fact and interpretation are the responsibility of the authors.

Abbreviations

AFMC	Air Force Materiel Command
BCAG	Boeing Commercial Airplane Group
CEO	chief executive officer
DD350	Individual Contracting Action Report
DLA	Defense Logistics Agency
DoD	Department of Defense
FY	fiscal year
GSA	General Services Administration
GSCM	global supply-chain management
HP	Hewlett-Packard
IBM	International Business Machines Corporation
MRO	maintenance, repair, and operations
OEM	original equipment manufacturer
PSM	purchasing and supply management
SBU	strategic business unit
SSG	Shared Services Group
UTC	United Technologies Corporation

CHAPTER ONE

The Increasing Importance of Supply Strategies

Throughout the past century, purchasing practices have become increasingly important to the overall success of enterprises (Fawcett, 2000).[1] Historically, purchasing has been viewed as a clerical function for ensuring short-term supply needs. External purchases of goods and services typically accounted for about 30 percent of an enterprise's budget.

As in the private sector, purchased goods and services are growing in importance for the Air Force and DoD because of competitive sourcing and the reengineering of processes for greater efficiency. Competitive sourcing is likely to increase the amount of purchased goods and services government procures in its efforts to embrace more competition, innovation, and choice. Reengineering or application of lean practices may mean fewer personnel are needed to do the same work because the replacement of "simple jobs and complex processes" with "complex jobs and simple processes" eliminates "non–value-added work [and the] jobs often go[ing] along with it" (Hammer, 1996, p. 231). Specific Air Force and DoD initiatives and operational challenges that will increase the importance of purchased goods and services include

- *Transformation Planning Guidance* to transform how DoD fights, does business, works with others, and manages uncertainty and operational turbulence, e.g., Sense and Respond Logistics (DoD, 2003)
- *Joint Vision 2020* focuses logistics requirements for precise, time-definite delivery (Joint Chiefs of Staff, 2000)
- *Air Force Transformation Flight Plan* and Agile Combat Support goals to be light, lean, and lethal, which require a responsive, reliable, and high-quality supply base that is not too large or unwieldy to manage (U.S. Air Force, Future Concepts and Transformation Division, 2003)

---

[1] By *enterprise*, we mean, as *Merriam-Webster's Collegiate Dictionary* defines the term, "a unit of economic organization or activity; esp[ecially] a business organization." We use this term to emphasize that, while many of the practices we describe were developed for private business, they are applicable to business processes for goods and services purchased by other organizations, including the Department of Defense (DoD). That is, their use need not be restricted to private-sector or nonprofit entities.

- Air Force goals to improve weapon system availability and reduce logistics and other support costs (U.S. Air Force, Directorate of Innovation and Transformation, 2004).

Finding better ways to manage its supply base, thereby improving flexibility and performance and reducing costs, is one way for the Air Force to meet these challenges. Many leading commercial enterprises have adopted innovative purchasing and supply management (PSM) practices to improve their quality, responsiveness, reliability, and flexibility while reducing costs (Moore et al., 2002). These practices have shifted PSM from managing items to managing suppliers and supplier capacity. These practices include

- analyzing enterprisewide spend[2]
- conducting market analyses and supply strategies
- reducing or consolidating the number of contracts with each supplier
- establishing long-term partnerships with the best suppliers
- working with the best suppliers to improve quality, cost, and service
- integrating key suppliers into systems, plans, processes, and organizations.

More strategic-sourcing initiatives—particularly for analyzing spend, conducting market analyses, reducing the number of contracts, and establishing partnerships with the best suppliers—are being mandated throughout the federal government. The Office of Management and Budget has charged each federal agency to identify at least three commodities that could be purchased more efficiently through strategic sourcing and to develop an agencywide strategic sourcing plan with performance measures, annual goals and objectives, and training for agency personnel to support strategic sourcing (Johnson, 2005). In addition, the Senate Armed Services Committee has recommended that each military department establish a Contract Support Acquisition Center to help achieve savings comparable to those civilian agencies have realized but that are more difficult for DoD because of its decentralization and its lack of an organization dedicated to making strategic sourcing decisions (U.S. Senate Committee on Armed Services, 2005).

This monograph synthesizes the literature on segmenting spend, prioritizing sourcing initiatives, developing supply strategies, and other related topics. It is written for Air Force and DoD leaders, managers, and personnel charged with overseeing or developing supply strategies. Because there is no empirical testing or consensus on any one process for targeting sourcing initiatives or developing a supply strategy, we consider multiple sources of evidence to outline a composite supply strategy development process drawing on the best of all literature to date.

---

2 This analysis would cover the total expenditures of an enterprise, as well as expenditures by commodity and supplier. Note that, in our context, the term *spend* refers to a given set of expenditures.

In Chapter Two, we document the evolution of purchasing from a tactical activity to a strategic function and define supply strategies and identify their key components. In Chapter Three, we discuss why supply strategies should be tailored to particular commodities. Chapter Four presents a composite process for segmenting, prioritizing, and targeting commodities for developing supply strategies enterprisewide. Chapter Five outlines how to develop and apply a supply strategy for specific goods and services across the enterprise. The final chapter reiterates some key points of our work and identifies ongoing initiatives of interest. At the end of the book are three appendixes. The first describes a process for grouping requirements; the second examines how commercial firms have organized their supply strategies; and the last lists prospective supply risks.

CHAPTER TWO

The Evolution of Purchasing

Historical Background

Purchasing first grew in importance for the military during World War II as the federal government purchased more weapons and goods to support troops. From the 1940s through the early 1970s, the private sector increasingly viewed purchasing as a managerial rather than a clerical function. This shift coincided with the increasing importance of purchasing to organizational expenditures. Among the contributors to this shift were decreasing expenditures for labor and overheads resulting from automation and more-efficient work processes and increasing expenditures for external resources resulting from easier access to world supply markets, the development of specialized contractors, and increasingly complex technologies that restricted the ability of organizations to make their own production inputs (Baily et al., 2005).

The importance of purchasing increased during the 1970s and early 1980s as shortages and inflation became more common. In the late 1980s and early 1990s, the competitive success of Japanese automotive companies and their close partnerships with suppliers to support just-in-time manufacturing pushed purchasing toward a strategic role, including the development of supply strategies. As a result, while purchasing and supply processes remained most concerned with obtaining the lowest prices for a commodity, there was a greater awareness of other contributors, such as quality and delivery, to the cost of a commodity, as well as more involvement between purchasers and suppliers and purchasers with other internal corporate functions (Baily et al., 2005).

In recent years, outsourcing trends have further increased the importance of purchasing practices as enterprises have sought to focus more on their core competencies. Today, many enterprises will spend up to 70 percent of their budgets on purchased goods and services. Purchasing and supply are increasingly seen as potential sources of strategic advantage for an organization. This new focus requires close collaboration with suppliers and entails greater concerns for total costs, including those incurred both before and after transactions, rather than just transaction prices (Baily et al., 2005).

Just as purchased goods and services have become increasingly important for private enterprises, so they have also grown in importance for public organizations, including the military. In recent decades, purchased goods and services, including procurement of weapons, have increased from 45 to 65 percent of the DoD budget, with the increase for nonweapon purchases being particularly steep (see Figure 2.1).[1]

Within the Air Force, purchased goods and services, including procurement of weapons, have increased from 67 to 71 percent of the budget in the past decade. In nominal dollars, the amount the Air Force spent on purchased goods and services, including procurement of weapons, increased from $49.6 billion in fiscal year (FY) 1996 to $93.1 billion in FY 2005.

The Shifting Focus of Purchasing Processes

Traditional purchasing processes were *reactionary*—a relatively linear process developed in reaction to a user's need. Baily et al. (2005) summarizes the main stages as follows:

- recognition of need
- specification
- make-or-buy decision
- source identification
- contracting
- contract management
- receipt and inspection
- payment
- fulfillment of need.

A user, for example, might identify a requirement for a good or service and ask purchasing personnel for help in obtaining it, usually as soon as possible. Sometimes, but not always, a user might identify possible sources for the good or service. The purchaser would then decide whether to make or buy the needed good or service and, if buying, how to do so.

More generally, requirements were generated by one function, e.g., engineering, item managers, or another ultimate user. They were then given to another function, e.g., contracting, purchasing, or another supply management function. Contracting, purchasing, or similar personnel procured the goods or services to meet the requirement and then turned it over to a third function to manage. Each of these groups of personnel typically had different objectives and measurements of performance, some

[1] In fact, procurement of weapons as a proportion of the DoD budget decreased during this time; the increase noted was all due to increased purchases of other goods and services.

Figure 2.1
DoD Expenditures for Procurement and Other Goods and Services, 1950 to 2005

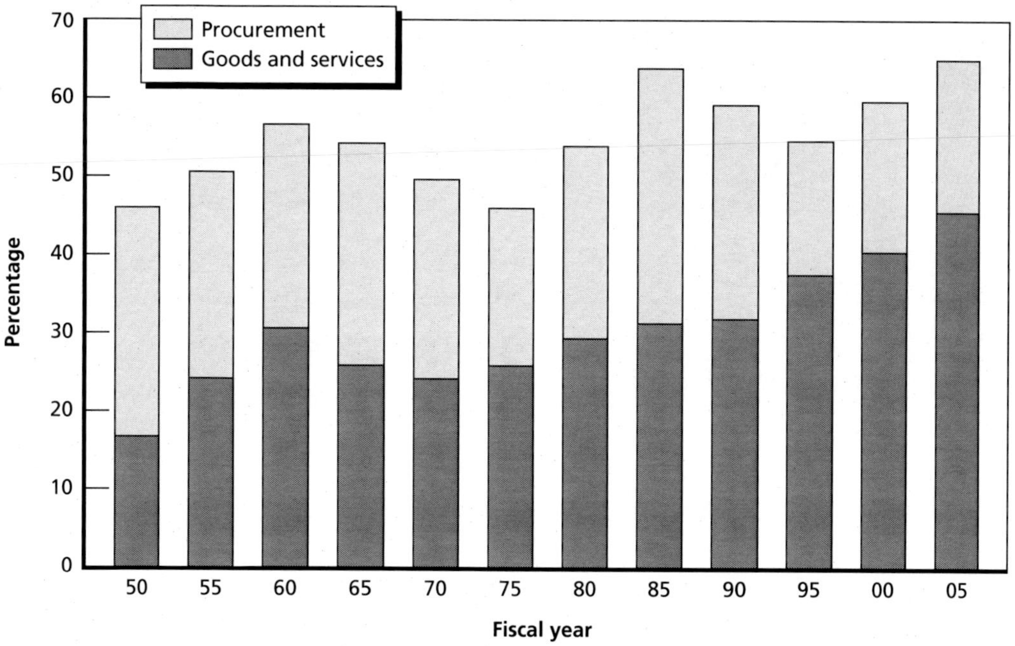

RAND *MG572-2.1*

of which can be at cross-purposes.[2] As a result, there was often no common focus throughout the purchasing process, poor information flow between steps of the process, and lengthy cycle times.

Traditional purchasing practices in the United States were criticized "for excessive focus on tactical functions," e.g., processing of purchase orders, verifying delivery status of missing items, and other activities contributing little to corporate profitability (Smock, 2004). A traditional purchasing department spent the bulk of its time on activities least likely to add value to an enterprise (Figure 2.2). It spent about three times as much time on "downstream" activities (activities occurring after contract placement, including inspection, monitoring and solving problems, invoice matching, and other paperwork task), than on "upstream" activities (activities occurring before contract placement, such as supply planning, development of contract strategy, and supplier selection), which are more likely to add value to an enterprise (Steele and Court, 1996). Failure to spend sufficient resources on upstream activities is a principal cause of large downstream workloads and costs and can cause an enterprise to

[2] See Mariotti (1999, particularly p. 75) on how cross-functional process issues within an organization are related to how the organization manages its supply chain. Purchasing managers, for example, seek low prices through large, infrequent orders, while inventory planners seek high inventory turnover to limit obsolescence of stock, which is achieved through smaller, more-frequent orders.

Figure 2.2
Purchasing Departments Typically Spent the Most Time on Activities Adding the Least Value

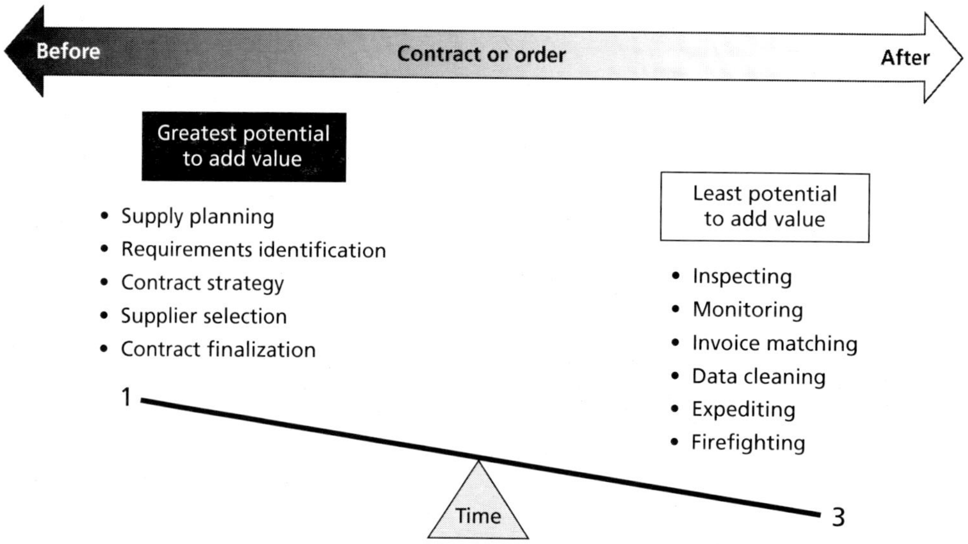

SOURCE: Developed from information in Steele and Court (1996).
RAND *MG572-2.2*

miss opportunities for improving overall performance and reducing costs and risks throughout the supply chain.

Developing a proactive supply strategy before a requirement must be met offers considerably more opportunities for performance improvement and total cost reductions than reactive purchasing. Because reactive purchasing typically has very short timelines and is executed at the operational level, it can do very little to

- aggregate similar or related requirements
- change the number, composition, or workload of suppliers
- adjust resource levels, capacity, or capability
- improve inventory mix, size, or location
- otherwise change purchasing policies, practices, operations, or organizations (Hicks, 2000).

Supply strategies developed before a requirement must be met and at the strategic (enterprisewide) level can be developed over a longer time and consequently can change anything in the supply process except customer requirements. As supply strategies shift from reactive and tactical to proactive and strategic, they shift focus from the lowest base or unit price for the commodity to the lowest total cost for the enterprise in providing the highest total value for the ultimate customer in the supply chain (Coyle, Bardi, and Langley, 2003).

U.S. corporations have increasingly recognized the need to develop supply strategies. A recent survey found most U.S. corporations have begun formal strategic sourcing programs, including reducing or overhauling their supply bases, and nearly all the remainder intend to start such programs (Smock, 2004). Such corporations are following the lead of Japanese automotive companies that have found that the key to high service levels and low total costs, including those related to quality and reliability, is often in working with a small number of carefully selected and closely integrated suppliers in longer-term relationships designed for continuous improvement (Dyer, Cho, and Chu, 1998).

Supply Strategies: Their Definition and Evolution

A *supply strategy* is a proactive means of acquiring and managing a group of goods or services. It outlines how the enterprise intends to ensure cost-effective, responsive, reliable, high-quality supplies to meet current and future needs.

A supply strategy should be developed *before* beginning the purchasing process. It is designed to serve not just one purpose or acquisition or just one business unit but to serve acquisition and management throughout the entire enterprise. It should be aligned with the strategic goals of the enterprise and should include the supply of materials; the suppliers and supply base for the materials; and, indeed, the end-to-end supply chain through which materials and supplies flow.

It typically covers a grouping of goods and services that can be related for various reasons (common suppliers, usage, technology, processes, etc.). It focuses both on short-term needs, such as ongoing production, and on long-term changes, such as the types of supplies and capacity likely to be needed in future years. A supply strategy evolves as enterprise needs change. That is, supply strategy development is iterative, with modifications as buyers learn and gather more information about their spend.

The literature on how to develop supply strategies is more diverse but less complete than that for the simpler process of purchasing and procurement. No standard or consensus process has emerged on exactly how to develop supply strategies. Given diverse products and industries, as well as the complexities of developing a supply strategy, it is not surprising that a simple, standard process is unlikely to fit all situations.

For the Air Force, supply strategies should encompass purchasing and logistics activities in the end-to-end supply chain, including the segments for weapon system maintenance, repair, overhaul, and modification, as well as delivery to the warfighter. The process should monitor both the "upstream" supply base, encompassing such goods and services as assemblies, subcomponents, parts, strategic raw materials, and repair services, and "downstream" to such end users as repair depots and operating units. For example, in purchasing to support the warfighter, the Air Force should look not just at the performance of a provider, such as Boeing or Lockheed, in supplying weapon systems to the warfighter but also at the supply bases for components, such as avionics and landing gear, and for builders of subcomponents for this equipment.

In many enterprises, purchasers traditionally look upstream, while logistics personnel look downstream. Developing a supply strategy that minimizes total costs while maximizing value to customers requires looking both upstream and downstream and taking the perspectives of a commodity (including, for example, supply base and suppliers), a product (including, for example, weapon systems), and customers.[3] The supply strategy to do so must be understood and communicated throughout the supply chain.

Changing Perspectives

Answering different supply questions often requires different perspectives and levels of analysis. For example, asking how well the supply strategy supports the customer might require analysis of mission capability. Answering questions on obtaining and assuring quality in the supply base requires a commodity perspective, with analysis of the number of contracts, total spend, and the number of quality suppliers for the commodity. Answering questions on how to better integrate and improve the supply chain requires a supplier perspective, with analysis of contract length, incentives, and past performance. Some questions, particularly those regarding commodities with more than one source, might require multiple perspectives. For example, answering questions on how to leverage spending may require both commodity and supplier perspectives. Using only one perspective is unlikely to lead to the best end-to-end result or even to identification of all questions that should be addressed.

Shifting to strategic PSM requires changes to four key elements of purchasing strategy (Fawcett, 2000): *objectives*, *resources*, *environment*, and *feedback*.

Objectives

Strategic PSM changes sourcing *objectives* from the traditional goals of reducing purchase price, minimizing administrative costs, and meeting internal customer needs to obtaining the lowest total cost of ownership and reengineering of purchasing and supply-chain processes while meeting ultimate customer needs. Reducing the total cost of ownership may mean an enterprise will pay more for a specific good or service under strategic purchasing than it would by traditional practices of purchasing.

One example of this is how Southwest Airlines maintains and overhauls its aircraft (B. F. Goodrich, 1997; A. T. Kearney, 2004). Because short flight turnaround

---

[3] In discussing *commodities*, we primarily use the definition of Flynn and Farney (2000, p. 151): "all goods and services purchased by an organization." Other authors that we synthesize use a narrower definition. Ellram and Choi (2000, p. 202) defines *commodities* as "homogeneous items that can be easily graded or classified . . . generally treated as raw materials" and available in a market that "closely resemble[s] pure competition."

times are essential to Southwest operations, the airline decided to perform all its own line maintenance, thereby reportedly improving turnaround time by 20 percent. By outsourcing its heavy maintenance, Southwest reportedly realized savings of 30 percent on engine maintenance, 18 percent on component repairs, and 15 percent on repairs for replaceable components.

In selecting an aircraft overhaul provider, though, Southwest did not select the cheapest provider but instead the provider that could provide the best quality work and help put aircraft back in service with the least downtime. It realized the lowest total cost for aircraft overhaul not by identifying the providers that might perform this service at the lowest price but those who helped it minimize all costs (including, for example, those related to aircraft unavailability) related to aircraft overhaul.

Resources

A shift to strategic PSM also requires a shift in *resources*. Traditional purchasing focuses on inputs (e.g., quantities purchased) and monitoring supplier performance. Strategic PSM focuses more on managing the capacity and developing the capabilities of suppliers, including "investments in knowledge, technology, and processes" (Fawcett, 2000, p. 13). One example of this is the development of the Wal-Mart inventory replenishment system, which combines human resources, technology, and the unique processes of Wal-Mart and its suppliers in a manner that would not be possible without extensive infrastructure support, including a fleet of company-owned trucks and a satellite system that directly links retail outlets, distribution centers, and suppliers. This system permits Wal-Mart and its suppliers to replenish its stores twice as often as its major competitors.

Environment

The *environment* for strategic PSM is broader than that for traditional purchasing. In the traditional purchasing environment, purchasing personnel reacted to external changes, which have been viewed as a challenge to overcome in maintaining traditional practices. In strategic PSM, proactive purchasing personnel view external changes as opportunities for the enterprise to exploit, particularly for leveraging relationships and technology to create customer value.

Feedback

Feedback is also more sophisticated for strategic PSM than for traditional purchasing. Traditional purchasing feedback focuses on monitoring supplier performance, with one-way information flows from users to the purchasing organization and from the purchasing organization to suppliers. Strategic PSM uses rigorous data analysis and two-way information flows to standardize and consolidate purchases and processes to help suppliers improve performance, to actively participate in product design, and to share ideas and information with customers and suppliers.

Improving Practices and Personnel Skills

Not only do objectives, resources, environment, and feedback change with the shift from traditional to strategic purchasing, but many individual practices change as well (Fawcett, 2000; Baily et al., 2005). Purchasing evolves from being a cost-center function to being a value-added function. Rather than reporting to some other corporate function, such as finance, purchasing reports to top management.[4] Product specification does not simply originate with the user but is developed between the user, purchasing organization, and supplier, as a means of considering all possible solutions to the user's needs.[5] Traditional purchasing organizations work with multiple suppliers, while strategic ones seek supply-base rationalization. Traditional purchasing organizations maintain their systems independently of suppliers, while strategic ones often integrate theirs with suppliers.

Strategic purchasing practices require personnel restructuring and training to execute successfully. In particular, as purchasing activities move from tactical to strategic, administrative functions are often automated, and the proportion of personnel with low skills is reduced, while the proportion of personnel with higher skills is increased.[6] As purchasing responsibilities change, the time allocations and functions of personnel change as well. A Booz Allen Hamilton survey showed purchasing personnel sharply increasing the time they devoted to supplier development, strategy, and analysis, while sharply curtailing the time they devoted to transactional buying and materials management (Laseter, 1998).[7] These changes, enabling more focus on areas likely to result

---

[4] A recent analysis of supply management and procurement innovation found that 89 percent of leaders in procurement innovation, but only 61 percent of other firms, assign their supply management organizations standing comparable to those of finance, marketing, and sales (A. T. Kearney, 2004). Similarly, 89 percent of leading firms, but only 58 percent of others, involve supply management in setting company strategy, and all leading firms, but only 63 percent of others, place senior procurement personnel on the executive management team of the company.

[5] For example, recent Procter & Gamble product innovations in skin care, dental, and household cleaning products resulted from supplier contributions, and half its product innovations in the baby care business unit are expected to come from suppliers (Rudzki et al., 2006; A. T. Kearney, 2004). Research at Alcoa on how consumers cool canned beverages at home led to Coca-Cola's development of the "Fridge Pack," which the company has credited with increasing canned soda sales by 10 percent (A. T. Kearney, 2004).

[6] This need not lead to greater total expenses. Nelson, Moody, and Stegner (2001) argues that the payback (i.e., annual realized cost reduction) for supplier development professionals in purchasing is three times their annual costs. That is, a fully developed and professionalized purchasing workforce can realize savings up to three times the costs of such a workforce.

[7] Although this survey is now dated, it remains the most direct measure we able to find of shifting priorities for the time of purchasing personnel. Specifically, it found that, between 1993 and 1998, purchasing personnel time devoted to

- Sourcing strategy and analysis increased from 19 to 27 percent (and was expected to increase to 33 percent by 2003).
- Supplier development increased from 13 to 20 percent (and was expected to increase to 28 percent).

in greater savings, are realized in part by supply base rationalization and application of e-procurement technology to automate administrative tasks.

There are many purchasing practices for better managing total costs and supplier relationships. Costs can be often be reduced by aggregating purchase volumes, rationalizing the number of suppliers, improving contract compliance with preferred suppliers, measuring and managing buyer and supplier performance, controlling inventories, and improving forecasting. Such practices can work best when customized or tailored to specific purchasing situations. We turn next to more-general reasons for tailoring supply strategies.

- Materials management decreased from 26 to 18 percent (and was expected to decrease to 14 percent).
- Transactional buying decreased from 56 to 37 percent (and was expected to decrease to 25 percent).

More-recent indicators show that "world-class procurement executives operate with 38 percent fewer staff than typical companies, show significantly improved cycle times, and reduced error rates," accomplishments they are able to realize through "spend[ing] 27 percent more than their peers on technology" (Business Wire, 2005). This helps them achieve "a cost per purchase order of $8.34, while typical companies spend . . . $19.99 per purchase order." As a result of these reduced expenditures of time and money on transactional tasks, "world-class procurement executives can drive their organization to focus more intensively on leveraging their spending more effectively through supplier rationalization, spend visibility and analysis, [and] aligning procurement with business strategy."

CHAPTER THREE

The Need to Tailor Supply Strategies

While supply strategies have many benefits, they need to be tailored both to the overall strategy of an enterprise and to specific goods and services or groupings of goods and services. One supply strategy will not fit all goods and services an enterprise purchases, particularly such large and varied enterprises as the Air Force and DoD.

Many different variables affect the need for and shape of supply strategies. Not all goods and services that an enterprise purchases are equally important to it. To cite an admittedly contrived example, the Air Force should not expend the same sophisticated effort on developing a strategy for office supplies that would be necessary for one for weapon systems. Rather, organizations should expend the greatest effort on supply strategies for the most complex and strategic goods and services.

Three key variables affect the need for and shape of supply strategies:

1. *The strategic importance of a group of goods or services to the enterprise and its customers* (Kraljic, 1983). The different goods and services that an enterprise purchases will vary in their effects on customers, technology, and performance. Production inputs will also vary in their effects on the profitability of the final products or reputation of an enterprise.
2. *The complexity and uncertainty of supply markets* (Kraljic, 1983). This includes the availability and performance of goods and services, the pace of technological change or material substitution, market-entry barriers, logistics costs and complexity, and the supplier market (monopoly, oligopoly, or competitive) and conditions (profitability, competition, future prospects, culture match with buyer). In a highly competitive market, some items, such as desktop computers that are in high demand, will not need a supply strategy that is as sophisticated as one for critical but slow-moving aircraft parts in a different market. Movement of industries overseas can also lead to complicated and expensive logistics and supply-chain complexities and risks that supply strategies must address.
3. *The complexity and uncertainty of an enterprise's customer requirements.* This includes the breadth of spend categories, as well as the level, variance, and stability of customer demands over time. A supply strategy for stable customer

demands (e.g., food) will likely differ from one for highly variable demands (e.g., parts that seldom fail).

We next review how these key variables affect efforts to tailor supply strategies to the strategic importance of the purchase, buying power of the purchaser, buyer and supplier cultures, available technology, and types of products.

Tailoring for Specific Characteristics

Strategic Importance of the Purchase

The strategic importance of purchases can affect both the value that can be added by a supply strategy and the nature and type of supplier relationship based on that strategy (Figure 3.1). At one extreme, goods that have little strategic importance and for which less value can be added through supplier relationships are often best handled through arm's-length relationships, with goods of least importance acquired through largely interchangeable vendors (Dobler and Burt, 1996). Traditional suppliers can suffice for adding value to supplier relationships for items of slightly greater strategic importance. Some suppliers in arm's-length relationships may eventually become "certified suppliers" that have undergone rigorous evaluation by the buyer and have demonstrated over time that they meet or exceed buyer criteria on cost, quality, or delivery (Leenders et al., 2002; Goldfeld, 1999). For items of the greatest strategic importance and for which supplier relationships might be expected to add the greatest value, more-sophisticated partnerships or strategic alliances are needed.

Figure 3.1
Strategic Importance of the Purchase Affects Optimal Choice of Supply Relationship

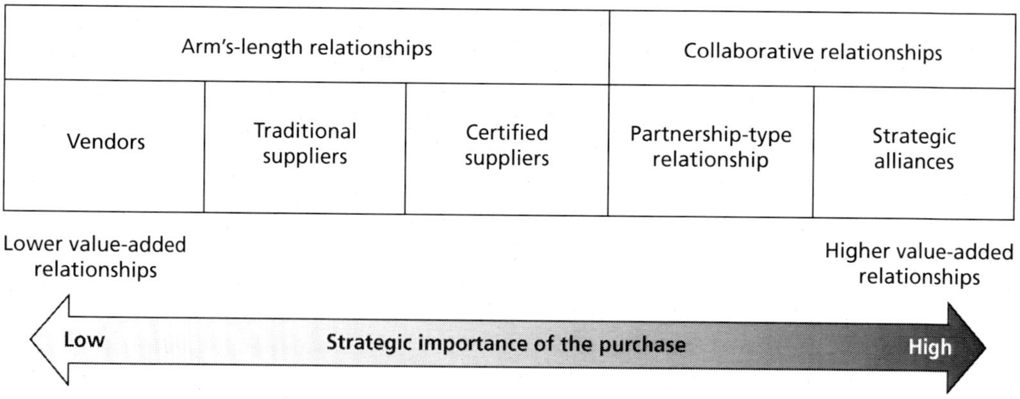

SOURCE: Dobler and Burt (1993). Copyright McGraw-Hill Companies, Inc. Used with permission.
RAND *MG572-3.1*

Supply strategies and the supplier relationships based on them need to reflect the breadth of goods and services an enterprise purchases. Enterprises purchasing wider varieties of goods and services need to tailor their supply strategies more heavily. Both the Air Force and DoD purchase an enormous variety of goods and services from several hundred different industries. In FY 2004, for example, contracting data indicate the Air Force purchased goods and services in 769 industries (as represented by North American Industrial Classification System codes), and DoD as a whole purchased goods and services in 1,111 different industries. Such a great breadth of goods and services, ranging from food to clothing to ammunition to fuel to weapon system parts, suggests that different Air Force and DoD supply relationships will likely require different supply strategies.

Buying Power of the Purchaser

The strategic importance of the purchase and buying power of the enterprise can also shape optimal operational characteristics of supplier relationships. Tang (1999) identifies four types of supplier relationships based on (1) the buying power of the enterprise and (2) the strategic importance of the purchase: *vendor*, *preferred supplier*, *exclusive supplier*, and *partner*. The buying power of the purchaser varies by ability to produce the parts, information or knowledge of the production process, supplier switching cost, the importance of the buyer to the supplier, the reputation of the buyer, and the number of suppliers in a market. In addition to the buying power of the enterprise and the strategic importance of the purchase, each may also differ by such characteristics as product specification and number of suppliers in the market.

For example, a purchaser with high buying power seeking a commodity of low strategic importance, for instance, a buyer purchasing a product such as standard hardware (such as nuts, bolts, screws, washers), may choose to do so through a *vendor* relationship. Such relationships are short term and typically executed through purchase orders in markets for standard products with many suppliers. They permit the enterprise to pressure the supplier to reduce costs and improve quality and responsiveness.

A purchaser with high buying power seeking a commodity of high strategic importance, for example, a buyer purchasing such products as unique spare parts needed for repairs in a market having relatively widespread knowledge of the general production process, may do so through a *preferred supplier* relationship. Such relationships are medium term (for example, the life of a product) and are typically executed through contracts in markets for specialized products with few suppliers. Such relationships require some involvement of senior management and frequent updates of cost, process, and quality information for the product from the supplier.

A purchaser with low buying power seeking a commodity of low strategic importance, for example, a buyer purchasing basic production materials for which few suppliers are available, may do so through an *exclusive supplier* relationship. Such relationships are medium term and are executed through contracts in markets for specialized products with only one or very few suppliers. Like preferred supplier relationships, these also require some senior management involvement and frequent information updates from the supplier but may also feature supplier development programs to help suppliers better meet buyer's needs.

A purchaser with low buying power seeking a commodity of high strategic importance, for example, a buyer purchasing materials or parts critical to its competitive edge but with few suppliers, such as those for high-technology weapon systems, may do so through a *partner* relationship. Such relationships are long term and are executed through agreements developed with the help of senior management for "leading edge" (such as new and innovative) products in markets with only one or very few suppliers. These also require continuous information from the supplier and feature supplier development programs.

Buyer and Supplier Cultures

Varying buyer and supplier cultures can affect the choice of supply strategies and relationships. Culture can be particularly important in tailoring strategies for purchasing services because buyer personnel and the supplier personnel who deliver services are likely to have considerable interaction.

Competitive strategies drive an enterprise's culture. A buyer that competes by offering the highest quality in its final product may not want to select a supplier that competes by offering low prices because its goods and services may not support the quality the buyer desires in its final product. A buyer with an "analytic" culture that places high value on measuring and assessing performance may not be compatible with a supplier with sloppy accounting practices.

The commitment of the buyer to a cooperative relationship and that of the supplier to competitive pricing will also affect the nature of the supply relationship (Laseter, 1998). Ideally, a high buyer commitment to a cooperative relationship and a high supplier commitment to competitive pricing can lead to a balanced sourcing strategy that fully leverages supplier capabilities and drives joint continuous improvement of both buyer and supplier.

Available Technology

Different levels of technology require different supply strategies. Buyers must consider the technology required for their needs and the degree of collaboration needed to develop it (Kaufman, Wood, and Theyel, 2000).

For commodities with high technology and high collaboration needs, buyers may seek a *problem-solving* supplier using advanced technologies and collaborative methods to promote innovation in products and processes (Kaufman, Wood, and Theyel, 2000). Such suppliers are less likely to emphasize cost and more likely to emphasize differentiation for commodities with small production runs and high process and labor flexibility.

For commodities with high technology but low collaboration needs, buyers may seek a *technology specialist* (Kaufman, Wood, and Theyel, 2000). By offering innovative products, such suppliers attract customers that seek but are not willing to invest in their own exceptional technology. Such firms may include proprietary parts suppliers whose technological innovations produce high barriers to market entry for other firms and that invest heavily in improving their own skills and assets.

Buyers may seek a *commodity supplier* for commodities with low technology and low collaboration needs (Kaufman, Wood, and Theyel, 2000). Such suppliers use standardized technology and work with customers through standard market contracts for spot buying or similar transactions.

For commodities with low technology but high collaboration needs, buyers may seek a *collaboration specialist* (Kaufman, Wood, and Theyel, 2000). Such suppliers use standardized technologies and skills to customize parts for buyers. That is, they supply goods requiring low levels of technology but high levels of collaboration between buyer and supplier.

Types of Products

Specific product characteristics also influence the choice of supply strategies. For example, commodities or standard parts with open architectures and cheap inputs for which there is likely to be very little interdependence between suppliers and buyers can be purchased through a *durable arm's-length* relationship, also called a *quasi-market* relationship (Dyer, Cho, and Chu, 1998). Commodities or parts that are nonstandard with closed architecture and requiring complicated inputs or multiple interactions between buyer and supplier, systems integration, or other features of high interdependence, should be purchased through *strategic partnerships*, also called *quasi-hierarchies*.

Strategic partnerships are necessary for "strategic" inputs—high-value commodities that are important in differentiating the buyer's final product and require a high degree of coordination between buyer and supplier (Dyer, Cho, and Chu, 1998). Organizational boundaries can blur for such quasi-hierarchies, which require multiple function-to-function interfaces between supplier and buyer. Suppliers in such relationships must be willing to make additional efforts for innovation and quality, such as specific investments in plant, equipment, personnel, and tailored resources.

For nonstrategic inputs, durable arm's-length relationships may suffice for executing supply strategies. Such relationships differ from traditional arm's-length relationships because initial supplier selection requires some benchmarking of capabilities to determine suppliers that have the potential for offering the lowest total costs over the long term. They also require the supplier and buyer to make some dedicated investments to facilitate their business (e.g., order entry, electronic data exchange, and logistics systems), and the buyer to assure the supplier of some future business as long as prices are competitive. Such a quasi-market approach can be superior to traditional arm's-length approaches because it minimizes procurement and transaction costs, allows suppliers to maximize economies of scale, and helps maintain vigorous competition.

Other Variables That Affect Tailoring of Supply Strategies

Several other variables not necessarily related to the purchased commodity also affect the strength of the supplier relationship and the ability of the enterprise to tailor supply strategies (Olsen and Ellram, 1997). Among these variables are current personnel skills, resources, and available time. The organizational structure of an enterprise and degree of enterprisewide coordination and cooperation affect the ability of the enterprise to establish cross-functional commodity teams. The current level of analytic rigor will likely affect the data, computational capabilities, and personnel available for developing supply strategies. The current thoroughness of documentation regarding supply relationships affects the ability of an enterprise to build on or expand past sourcing efforts. The number and quality of suppliers, level of supplier management, and sophistication of supply-chain design also affect the ability of an enterprise to make significant changes.

The research showing that the product, technology, strategic importance of the purchase, buying power of the purchaser, and the culture of the buyer and supplier affect the quality of a supply relationship demonstrate that a "one-size-fits-all" approach will not work for developing supply strategies. Instead, each commodity and supplier should be analyzed to determine the extent to which it contributes to the core competence and competitive advantage of the enterprise. All these affect the need for a supply strategy, as well as how suppliers and their contributions should be classified. In Chapter Four, we will review the steps enterprises must consider in devising a supply strategy, including the skills and abilities they must foster to develop one.

CHAPTER FOUR

Developing a Supply Strategy: Assessing and Prioritizing Enterprisewide Opportunities

Explicit processes for segmenting a business's spend are not new, but documented procedures for developing optimal supply strategies for those segments largely are. The first published supply strategy development process and segmentation framework appears to be that of Kraljic (1983). This work serves as the foundation for many later processes and segmentation frameworks (Gelderman and van Weele, 2005). Several additional processes and frameworks have been introduced in the past decade for segmenting goods, services, and suppliers and developing supply strategies.

These processes and analytic frameworks differ somewhat but also have some commonality, with the same or similar steps occurring in more than one framework. This permits us to present a composite supply strategy development process.

There are two primary phases in our composite:

- Phase I: Assess, group, segment, and prioritize enterprisewide opportunities
  1. Assign an enterprisewide, cross-functional team to group, segment, and prioritize spend (determining enterprise expenditures by commodity and supplier).
  2. Document and analyze purchases and spending by category groups or subgroups.
  3. Document current supply base and identify prospective risks.
  4. Segment and classify purchases by strategic importance and other factors.
  5. Identify and quantify prospective opportunities.
  6. Assess capabilities and ease of internal and external execution.
  7. Prioritize opportunities by expected benefit and effort.

- Phase II: Develop supply strategies for pilots/commodity group initiatives with greatest value and fastest payback
  8. Assign and resource a cross-functional team to each selected commodity group.
  9. Develop a more-detailed profile of the selected commodity groups.

10. Analyze the industry and supply market for a selected commodity group.
11. Identify and prioritize prospective risks and vulnerabilities.
12. Develop a strategy.
13. Execute the strategy.

Phase II, reviewed in Chapter Five, includes commodity initiatives tailored to particular needs and ideally selected for the size and speed of their expected business effects (the extent to which they might contribute to the strategic goals of an enterprise) and payback (the return expected in proportion to the resources, time, effort, and risks necessary to attain the benefits). The first phase involves a general, high-level overview to identify broad areas of spend for "triage," or prioritization based on which PSM initiatives can be expected to yield the greatest returns, including where automation of noncritical purchases may free personnel for other, more-critical acquisitions. The second requires both greater overall and more-detailed effort to design and implement initiatives for individual groups of goods and services, in turn requiring a finer, more in-depth level of analysis.

Phase I, reviewed in this chapter, the opportunity assessment phase of developing supply strategies, may include an enterprisewide spend analysis to document current purchases and suppliers (Eversbusch, 1998). The total buy identified by such analysis can then be grouped into categories of spending. Such categories may, for example, include those purchased from a particular Product Service Code or Federal Supply Class, from a particular industry, or related to a weapon system. This analysis should be guided by the goals and objectives of the enterprise. Grouping spending categories can help identify opportunities for leveraging economies of scale and scope. Relevant employees, particularly those with broad knowledge of various spending categories, should be identified and involved in the enterprisewide process of grouping total spending into each major category. Once spending groups have been identified, each can be segmented, and opportunities for applying strategic sourcing can be identified and prioritized. This first phase of developing a supply strategy emphasizes breadth more than rigor in its high-level analysis.

Step 1: Assign an Enterprisewide Cross-Functional Team to Group, Segment, and Prioritize Spend

Before assessing and prioritizing potential opportunities for improved PSM, the first step is to establish an enterprisewide, cross-functional team to conduct or oversee analyses of spend, markets, industries, and suppliers and to develop and validate category groups or subgroups for segmenting and prioritizing spending. Team members should be selected for their ability to assess opportunities across the enterprise, that is, to develop and validate enterprisewide spend category groups or subgroups by product, commodity, or service; to position spend in a portfolio matrix showing, for example, how commodities compare by value to the enterprise and difficulty in procurement; and to assign priorities to categories for supply strategy initiatives.

Team members may include personnel from such functions as purchasing, engineering, manufacturing, customer relations, supplier relations, logistics, finance, quality control, and legal affairs. In particular, Goldfeld (1999) recommends including personnel from key functional areas to provide many different perspectives on each commodity, its end product, and its reasons for market success (e.g., price, quality, technology), as well as the functions that can provide funds and staffing for implementing selected strategies. Team members with seniority, tenure, and breadth of knowledge regarding enterprise operations can be particularly valuable members of this team. Some team members will work on team activities full time; some will do so part time; and some will do so occasionally, as needed.

Step 2: Document and Analyze Enterprisewide Purchases and Spend by Category Groups or Subgroups

Once an enterprisewide, cross-functional team is in place, it should conduct or lead a *spend analysis*—an analysis of the total amount an enterprise spends to obtain goods and services and of expenditures by commodity, supplier, and other categories. A spend analysis evaluates categories of expenditures by dollar value, number and types of contracts, contract terms, purchasing organizations, and frequency of purchases. A spend analysis should also evaluate spending by industry, parent company, location of suppliers and deliveries, supply risks, and other relevant spending variables. For federal agencies, such as DoD and the Air Force, other relevant variables may include goals for spending with small and disadvantaged businesses. Spend analyses should, if possible, examine not just historic patterns but likely future patterns for various goods and services.[1]

In sum, a spend analysis should identify key indicators for prospective opportunities to reduce costs or improve performance using best PSM practices, as well as prospective supply risks. The opportunities it identifies may include possibilities to leverage buying power by identifying corporate family relationships and other interrelated suppliers, as well as duplicate suppliers (two or more suppliers providing the same good or service). A spend analysis can also be used to measure compliance with preferred vendor programs. Among the risks to procurement that a spend analysis can help identify are those indicated by a single supplier or limited competition with few bidders, low or highly variable demand, and no contract in place for a good or service. With sufficient manpower and resources, a spend analysis can also identify such risks

[1] For an example of a spend analysis for the Air Force, see Moore et al. (2004).

as a lack of supplier performance incentives or commitment to improvement, inadequate or poor past performance information, and inappropriate scopes of work for some suppliers.

A spend analysis should begin with an enterprisewide extraction of spending and related data from all available internal and external systems. An effective spend analysis requires aggregation of spending data into a single consolidated view of spend (Aberdeen Group, 2002).[2] Spending data should be categorized as much as possible at the level of individual items or services to provide visibility and allow comparisons of detailed attributes across suppliers and commodities. The data should also enable a precise view of spending with each supplier and for each commodity by the entire enterprise, as well as by each of its divisions, sites, and individual buyers, and should allow comparisons of price and such other attributes as inflation, contract compliance, and premium cost variance.[3]

Among the barriers that can impede a spend analysis are the following (Aberdeen Group, 2002):

- dispersion of spend data across multiple sources
- vague, inconsistent, or erroneous item data
- inconsistent product or supplier names[4]
- limited analysis and strategy capabilities.

Attempting to address these barriers can be time-consuming and laborious. Nevertheless, spend data validation, cleansing, enhancing, and analysis can help overcome these barriers over time. The resolution of spend analyses can be improved by incorporating into these cyclical processes business rules for recognizing, resolving, and classifying similar data in the future.

Enterprises gaining full visibility into consolidated and actionable spending information may uncover, on average, opportunities to reduce total spending by 2 to 10 per-

---

2 While complete and accurate data are desirable, an enterprise does not have to document 100 percent of its spend or have perfect data to use the information to make improvements. It can be better "to get something done" in some areas rather than to expend considerably more time and energy to ensure total accuracy (Duffy, 2005, p. 5).

3 Examples of other nonprice data useful for a spend analysis include internal enterprise data on buyer and supplier profiles, part descriptions, bills of materials, part-usage trends, tooling information, purchase order and invoice history, inventory status, commodity attributes, procurement and production plans, performance, site information, and routing data. Useful external data would include commodity and market trends; industry spending patterns; lead times; and "parent-child" relationships between supplier companies, divisions, and sites (Aberdeen Group, 2002).

4 Often an enterprise assigns multiple part numbers to a single product and gives different names or abbreviations in different systems to a single vendor. Such disparities must be reconciled so that spending data can be classified by a common taxonomy and to a level of detail that is meaningful for analysis (Aberdeen Group, 2002). The Federal Procurement Data System–Next Generation central contractor registry represents an attempt to improve supplier data for federal government purchases by standardizing supplier information.

cent (Aberdeen Group, 2002). Without full visibility into all the enterprise's purchasers and suppliers, fewer opportunities for savings may be possible. Still, even when ideal data are not readily available, the data that are available can often provide insights on where to target further analysis and spend initiatives.

Within the Air Force, DD350 form data, though not optimal for a spend analysis, can help in compilation of a first-order spend analysis. These data, now collected on individual contract actions of at least $3,000, provide information by major category (Federal Supply Class, Product Service Code, or North American Industry Classification code, rather than by individual item) on purchases comprising 97 percent of all Air Force direct purchases. The data also include how much and what the contract was for, the purchase office issuing the contract, the name of provider winning the contract, the industry classification of purchases, the numbers of solicitations and offers (indicating some market conditions), and the types of contracts (e.g., sole-source or competitive). Such information can suffice for a preliminary, high-level analysis of Air Force spend (Moore et al., 2004; however, see also Dixon et al., 2005, on problems in such data).

Even a high-level spend analysis can illustrate prospective opportunities to leverage purchases and persuade senior management to allocate resources for implementing new purchasing, supply, and supply-chain management practices and to create a new PSM organization or significantly restructure the existing one. A high-level spend analysis can also be used to identify areas of prospective high procurement risk and administrative costs, to group and segment spend, and to help identify or target prospective spend areas for initiatives in PSM (particularly those most likely to deliver significant rewards and performance improvements in a reasonable amount of time with minimal risks). While a high-level analysis can help identify many issues to consider in developing supply strategies, a more-complete spend analysis for a particular group of goods or services may be required before implementing many new elements of a new supply strategy.[5]

Step 3: Document Current Supply Base and Identify Prospective Risks

In addition to its spend, a buyer should also document its total number of suppliers, the portfolio of products it purchases, and the performance of suppliers providing these. Suppliers should also be documented by geography (for example, the vulnerability of suppliers to natural disasters or political events), dependency (the percentage of a supplier's business associated with a particular buyer as well as the percent of a given

---

[5] This analysis would include information on the needs, preferences, and priorities of the ultimate users of commodities, as well as the reasons for current purchasing practices; see Chapter Five.

commodity for a buyer that a supplier provides),[6] logistics costs (for example, transportation time and costs, risks of disruptions or delays), and other policy variables that may be of concern to the buyer (for example, the federal mandate to support small and disadvantaged businesses). In the previous step, the enterprisewide team documents and analyzes enterprisewide purchases by category groups and subgroups to assess how the enterprise spends its money for a major category group or subgroup; in this step, the team gathers more high-level information on suppliers and the industry external to the enterprise. The previous step focuses inward, on the enterprise's current spending and spending history; this step looks outward, to suppliers and into the future to identify and execute opportunities to improve supply performance.

Regarding dependency, a buyer that accounts for a high percentage of business for a particular supplier may have more leverage with that supplier than it otherwise would.[7] Conversely, a buyer dependent on one supplier for a particular commodity may find itself with less leverage than it otherwise might have. Such evaluations also help identify risks the buyer may face from variations in supply availability, costs, and performance, including possible problems resulting from irregular or late deliveries and those resulting from commodity defects.[8]

Step 4: Segment and Classify Purchases by Strategic Importance and Other Factors

Once a spend analysis is complete and the supply base has been documented, purchases should be segmented by value, volume, risks, and other variables that can affect

---

6 The dependency of a supplier on a buyer can be calculated by dividing the total spend of a buyer with a supplier by the total sales of the supplier. For many suppliers, information on total sales can be found in filings with the Securities and Exchange Commission or through business information offered by such firms as Dun & Bradstreet.

7 At the same time, buyers may not want suppliers to become too dependent on them. According to Dobler and Burt (1996, pp. 224–225),

> Many highly regarded firms try not to be more than 15 to 25 percent of any one supplier's business. They reason that if their purchases represent too large a share of the supplier's business and they discontinue a product or purchase an item from another supplier, they could put the supplier in a very difficult financial situation.

Similarly, Burt and Pinkerton (1996, p. 117), while noting exceptions for strategic alliances and single and sole-source suppliers, notes that

> If [a buyer's] purchases appreciably exceed 20 percent or so [of a supplier's business], the purchaser begins to assume a moral responsibility for the economic well-being of the supplier. The purchaser loses needed flexibility in such a situation and may find itself morally committed to a supplier who is no longer competitive or capable of performing the desired services.

8 Using a single source of supply increases risk (Bowersox, Closs, and Cooper, 2002). Therefore, supply base reduction programs are almost always accompanied by rigorous supplier screening, selection, and certification. Contingency plans can also reduce the consequences of supply failure.

the performance of the enterprise. The first task here is to group purchases into relevant categories. Many enterprises begin by grouping their total spend requirements into two major categories: (1) direct spend for goods and services that are direct inputs to production processes, such as raw materials, parts, components, and major assemblies, and (2) indirect spend for goods and services that are not direct inputs to production processes, such as office supplies, information technology and telecommunications, travel, facilities, overhead and support, benefits and insurance, and maintenance, repair, and operations (MRO). These major spending categories may be further divided into smaller commodity groups or subgroups or even specific goods or services defined by industry (such as chemicals, metals, electronics), technology (such as machined parts, semiconductors), suppliers (such as facilities management or logistics services), or total spend (such as significant spending for a particular good or service). Each category of requirements should be large enough (either in absolute size or in comparison to all expenditures) to warrant the significant resources that would be used to develop a supply strategy for it. (See Appendix A for more on grouping requirements in developing supply strategies.)

Grouping and then segmenting goods, services, and suppliers with similar key attributes into different categories can help better link the best strategies, tactics, and management approaches for various goods and services to the overall goals of an enterprise (Carter, 1999).

Once an enterprise decides to segment its supply or suppliers, it must decide how to do so. The difficulty for an individual firm lies in determining the optimal measures to use in the segmentation process and in deciding where to focus its analytical effort. Two key segmentation frameworks are used commercially: Pareto (also known as ABC) analysis and portfolio analysis or supply positioning and segmentation. Although, as we will discuss, portfolio analysis offers more advantages than Pareto analysis does, they can be used in conjunction with each other to segment spend properly.

Pareto Analysis

Pareto analysis is based on the dollar volume of purchased goods and services, business per supplier, or inventory per item.[9] Specific dollar volumes are then divided into three (or more) classification levels (Figure 4.1). A Pareto analysis typically reveals that about 20 percent of the items and services that an enterprise purchases account for about 80 percent of its purchasing dollars and that about 20 percent of its suppliers provide the

---

[9] *Pareto analysis* is named for Vilfredo Pareto, an economist who observed that 80 percent of Italy's wealth was held by 20 percent of the population. His observation led economists more generally to focus on small concentrations that might have broader disproportionate effects. ABC (Pareto) analysis, for example, divides goods and services into "A," "B," and "C" categories, and focuses attention on the "A" category, which represents the 10 to 20 percent of goods and services that may account for 70 to 80 percent of purchase dollars. Whether called Pareto or ABC analysis, the goals of such segmentation are virtually the same: to identify relatively small concentrations of goods and services that have disproportionate effects on total spend.

Figure 4.1
Pareto Analysis Segments Spend by Dollars and Volume

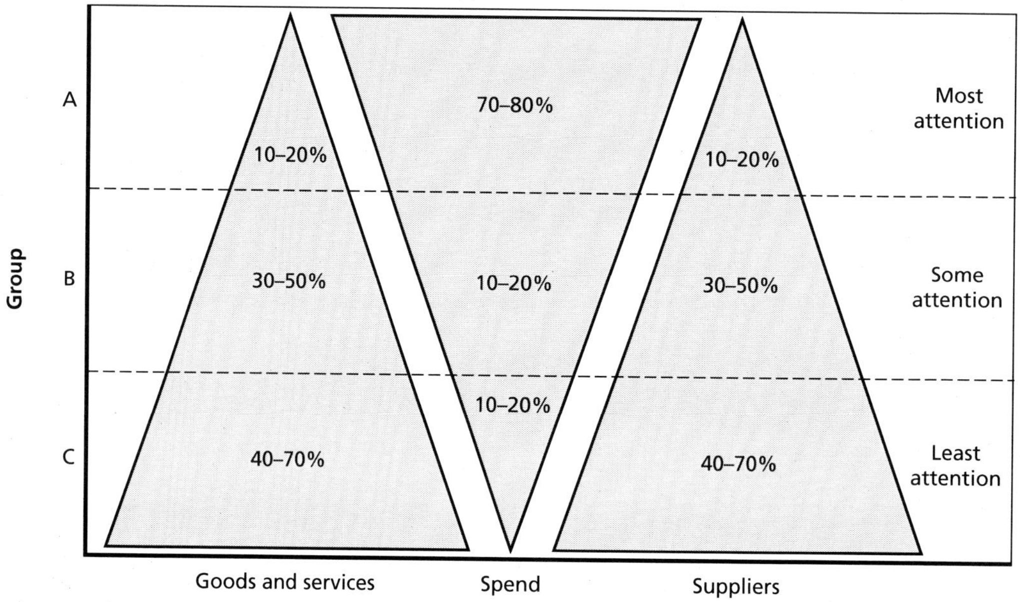

NOTE: The numbers here are ranges, so the extremes will not sum to 100 percent. The actual numbers will also vary by industry.
RAND *MG572-4.1*

goods and services that are most important to it (Carter, 1999). Enterprises typically pay the most attention to this top "A" group and the least to a bottom "C" group comprising the bulk of goods and services and the suppliers providing them but constituting a small proportion of overall expenditures.

In some cases, 50 percent of the goods and services that an organization purchases account for less than 2 percent of its spend (Steele and Court, 1996). Such dispersion of spend means that little effort need, or should, be spent on the bulk of all orders, given that most orders will have no significant influence on costs or profits and that concentrating on the goods and services of highest value will influence cost and profit the most. Figure 4.2 illustrates the concept. The goods and services represented by shaded areas B and C constitute 80 percent of the orders for an enterprise but only 20 percent of the cumulative spend. Therefore, for these commodities, a 10-percent price reduction would save 2 percent of total expenditures. The goods and services represented by shaded area A, on the other hand, constitute 20 percent of the orders but 80 percent of the spend. Thus, for these commodities, a 5-percent price reduction would save 4 percent in total expenditures. (See Steele and Court, 1996.)

Pareto segmentation can help enterprises prioritize their supply strategy efforts in areas that are likely to yield the greatest returns, such as inventory control, forecasting, and timing (Carter, 1999). In particular, by helping identify the goods and suppliers

Figure 4.2
Notional Example of Purchasing and the Pareto Curve

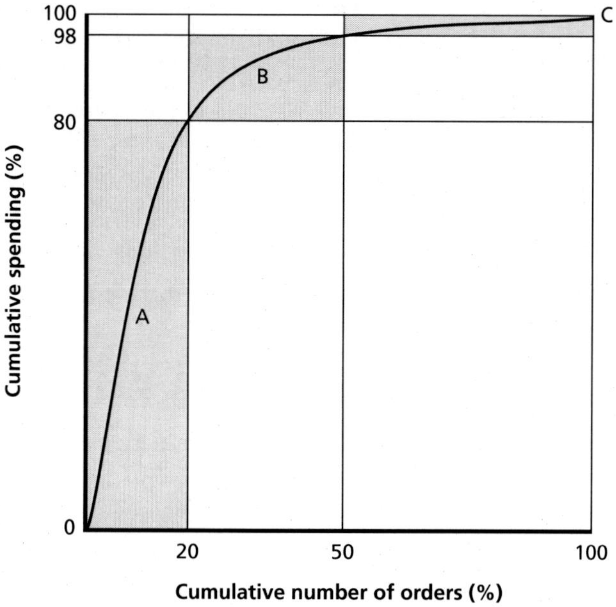

SOURCE: Steele and Court (1996). Copyright McGraw-Hill Companies, Inc. Used with permission.
RAND *MG572-4.2*

on which an enterprise spends the most money, a Pareto analysis can help an organization direct its resources toward the strategic purchases for which it might realize greater savings or performance improvements (Syson, 1992).

A Pareto analysis can also help identify areas in which an enterprise may wish to consolidate a very large number of small (say, less than $250) orders (Syson, 1992). Reducing these, even those accounting for a small percentage of total spend, can help reduce transaction costs, particularly administrative ones. (Indeed, for many small purchases, transaction costs can exceed the purchase price.)

While a Pareto analysis helps set priorities, it fails to account for many characteristics of the purchasing decision, such as the relative importance of goods and services or the tactics and strategies necessary for a particular market or supplier (Steele and Court, 1996). In particular, Pareto analysis

- fails to identify the low-value items that, if they fail or are not available, can have a disproportionate effect on a product and its profitability
- fails to discriminate between methods that could be used to obtain high-value goods and services subject to varying levels of product availability, number of suppliers, and criticality to the operation by focusing on purchase price, the most visible elements of cost, may miss elements that account for up to half the total cost

of ownership, including *pretransaction costs* in preparing for the purchase (such as identifying needs and qualifying sources), *transaction costs* in addition to price (such as delivery, billing, inspection, and return costs), and *posttransaction* costs (such as inventory, warehousing, maintenance, and repair costs).[10]

Examining the total cost of ownership offers the opportunity to identify areas for collaboration that reduce acquisition and supply-chain costs (Laseter, 1998). Because value can be hard to define and measure, costs should be quantified whenever possible. Responsiveness, for example, should be evaluated against the cost needed to achieve it. Some of the most cost-competitive companies often both provide superior service and low cost because they have adopted lean manufacturing and other processes that eliminate waste and enhance responsiveness.

Portfolio Analysis—Supply Positioning and Segmentation

The limitations of Pareto analysis for identifying the total cost of ownership and other variables affecting supply-chain performance have led to the development of additional methods that can be used with or independently of Pareto analysis. *Portfolio analysis*, also called *supply positioning* and *segmentation*, can help identify risks when determining resource allocations (Flynn and Farney, 2000).

Portfolio analysis segments spend by measures of vulnerability and value. Such analysis has its roots in the work of RAND Corporation analyst Harry Markowitz, who hypothesized that rational investors will select "efficient" portfolios that maximize returns for a given level of risk, quantifying the relationship between risk and return on investments (Markowitz, 1952; Turnbull, 1990). Today, purchasing portfolio models are a hallmark of more-sophisticated purchasing organizations, where the purchasing function is more likely to report directly to top management, contribute to the competitive position of an enterprise, and be staffed by cross-functional teams able to develop competitive strategies for the enterprise (Gelderman and van Weele, 2005).

Purchasing portfolio models must be used carefully. In reviewing the ways portfolio models have been used in strategic decisionmaking to support resource allocation decisions, Olsen and Ellram (1997) also notes several precautions. When using portfolio analysis for making purchasing decisions, it is important to consider the complexity of the dimensions used to categorize the elements of the portfolio. If the dimensions are very complex, an enterprise may focus too much on developing measures and categorizing elements. If the dimensions are too simple, important variables may be overlooked. Buyers must also balance needs for generalization and detail. Too much generalization can lead to overlooking important details of particular commodities,

---

[10] Riggs and Robbins (1998) reports that the purchase price alone represents only about 25 to 40 percent of the total cost to manage the acquisition and use of purchased goods and services, that is, the total cost of ownership. For more on total cost of ownership, see, among others, Ellram and Siferd (1998); Coyle, Bardi, and Langley (2003); and Bowersox, Closs, and Cooper (2002).

while too much detail can lead to overlooking relationships between commodities. Portfolio models can offer generic strategies, but businesses using them still require careful analysis of their feasible strategic options and execution, as we will discuss in Chapter Five (Day, 1986; Derkinderen and Crum, 1984).

Still, portfolio models, particularly if combined with other tools, including Pareto analysis, can be used to organize information, classify items in the portfolio, and improve allocation of limited resources by identifying which groups of goods and services, suppliers, or relationships warrant the most attention (Olsen and Ellram, 1997). In particular, portfolio analysis, because it considers risk, is an improvement over one-dimensional Pareto analysis. Supply risk or vulnerability can be assessed by, among other variables, commodity availability, number of suppliers, competitive demand, make-or-buy opportunities, storage risks, and substitution possibilities, while value or profit impact can be determined by the volume purchased, percentage of total spend devoted to the commodity, and effect on product quality or business growth (Kraljic, 1983).

Another approach to portfolio analysis considers goods by their relative cost, for example, their proportion of the total expenditures of an organization, and their vulnerability, as determined, for example, by limited availability, high quality requirements, and safety or environmental issues (Steele and Court, 1996). Differing commodities or buyer goals may warrant different segmentation criteria. Specific goods and services within a group may have varying characteristics dictating different supply strategies.

The supply positioning and segmentation process (portfolio analysis) has six steps, some of which (such as selecting a cross-functional team to lead the process) parallel those of the overall supply strategy process (Goldfeld, 1999). The team that conducts the opportunity assessment of the first phase of the supply development process typically conducts the supply positioning and segmentation process as well. Its steps are as follows:

- **Selecting a cross-functional team to lead the process.** This team is first assigned to group, segment, and prioritize spend.
- **Selecting commodity groups to position.** This should be selected from a list of all goods and services purchased by the enterprise (compiled in analyzing purchases and spend by category groups and subgroups in the overall supply strategy process).
- **Determining the requirements for the enterprise or business unit.** This can be determined from past and projected spending for all goods and services purchased by an enterprise.
- **Estimating the vulnerability and value of the commodity group.** Vulnerability and value can be determined from documentation and analysis of purchases and spend by category groups and subgroups and of the current supply base and

the prospective risks in it. Much of the work for this step is similar to steps 2 and 3 of the first phase of the overall process, discussed above.

- **Positioning the commodity, based on its vulnerability and value, within a segmentation or position matrix.** The team can do this by plotting items on axes representing relative vulnerability and cost.
- **Updating with shifts in supply markets and buying patterns.** Suppliers may enter or leave markets continuously, causing changes in the dynamics that buyers face, including, for example, supply vulnerability for a commodity.

The process of categorizing items can be even more important than the classification itself (Olsen and Ellram, 1997). During the process of categorization, team members must discuss inconsistencies and agree on the importance of commodity groups, suppliers, and relationships that are classified.

Still, the focus of this process is on the determination of relative vulnerability and value for commodity groups, then positioning them on a supply segmentation matrix (shown notionally in Figure 4.3). Products with low value and low vulnerability will appear in the lower left of a notional segmentation, while those with high value and high vulnerability will appear in the upper right.

The value of the purchase may be determined by its business benefits or its strategic importance. The strategic importance in particular is determined by competence, economic, and image issues (Olsen and Ellram, 1997). *Competence issues* include the relevance of the commodity group to the purchasing firm's core competencies (for instance, its technical advantages or specialized investments). *Economic issues* include the importance of the purchase to the total spend of the buying enterprise, to the final value added to the enterprise's product and to its profitability, to the future business growth of the firm, and to leveraging total spend with the supplier. *Image issues* include the importance of the commodity group to the image of the enterprise among its customers and suppliers, as well as the effects it may have on environmental and safety issues.

Vulnerability may also be determined by the degree of supply difficulty, procurement risk, and supply market complexity for a particular commodity. It may be determined by product characteristics, the supply market, and the supply environment. *Product characteristics* relevant to positioning include the novelty and availability of the good or service and its complexity, as determined by such variables as its specifications, number of parts or components, use and manufacturing processes, and storage risks, as well as any political variables that may affect its acquisition or use. *Supply market characteristics* include supplier power, as shaped by the size of the supplier, the number of suppliers and buyers in the market, dependence of the buying enterprise on both the commodity and the product, and the lack of appropriate substitutions; the technical and business competence of suppliers; and the opportunities the buying enterprise has to make or buy the good or service. *Supply environment characteristics* include such risks

Figure 4.3
Notional Supply Positioning

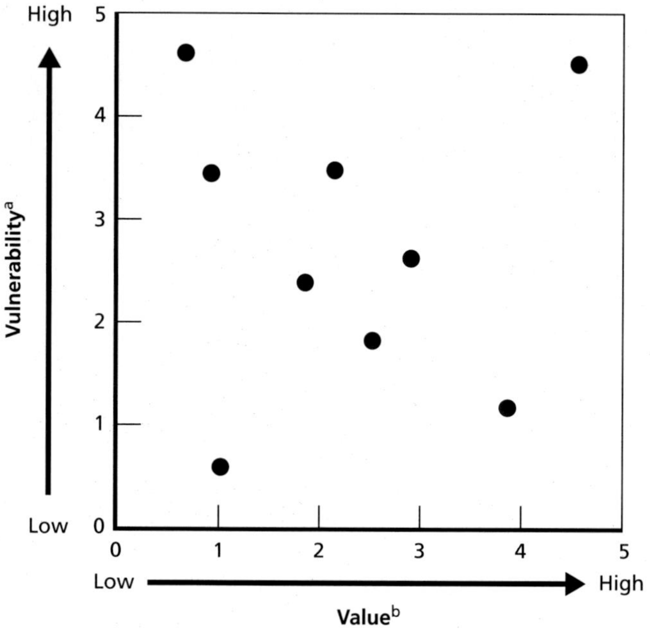

SOURCE: Adapted from Steele and Court (1996).
[a]In terms of risk, exposure, or strategic importance.
[b]In terms of influence or potential influence on profits and of relative cost as a total percentage of annual expenditures.
RAND *MG572-4.3*

and uncertainties as those related to opportunistic behavior by suppliers and technological changes.

Not all factors related to value and vulnerability in supply segmentation will apply to every purchase. Other factors not listed may apply. Nevertheless, the factors discussed above are representative of those that analysts should consider in a segmentation process.

Once groups of goods and services have been positioned according to their relative value and vulnerability, the matrix can be divided into quadrants. The purchasing goals and objectives will typically differ for each quadrant, as will the strategies and tactics, resources, personnel skills, and information technology needed for acquiring goods and services in each quadrant. Although strategies within quadrants are largely similar, supply strategies will also vary within each quadrant by the goals of the enterprise, the level of the enterprise spending, and the situation of suppliers and the supply market.

Goods of low value and low vulnerability may be referred to as *noncritical* (the term we use), *generic*, *tactical*, or *acquisition* items. Those with high value but low vulnerability may be called *leverage* (the term we use) or *commodities* or *tactical profit* items. Those with low value but high vulnerability may be called *bottleneck* (the term we use), *critical*, or *strategic security* items. Those with high value and high vulnerability may be called *strategic* (the term we use), *strategic critical*, or *strategic partnership* items. The names of axes for these quadrants differ as well. As noted earlier, *vulnerability* (the term we use) may be referred to as *degree of supply difficulty*, *difficulty of managing purchase*, *procurement risk*, and *supply market complexity*, among other names. *Value* (the term we use) may be referred to as *business impact*, *financial impact*, *relative cost*, and *strategic importance of purchase*. (See Figure 4.4 for a more complete listing of names for each quadrant and the academic and professional users of each name.)

The exact names for each quadrant are not vital here and are shown only to link differing perspectives on the same topics. We review characteristics of each of these quadrants below to provide an overview of what practitioners and researchers have done in the past. The goals, spend, and supply market for any specific enterprise and its commodities may vary considerably from these generalized situations.

Noncritical. *Noncritical* commodities, with low vulnerability and low value, typically include such goods and services as office supplies, furniture, vehicles, building maintenance, travel services, and equipment MRO (Figure 4.5).

The market for these commodities is usually highly competitive, with abundant standardized supplies available from many local and global suppliers (Figure 4.6). Such goods and services have no special availability, quality, safety, reliability, or environmental issues associated with them and typically comprise a large proportion of the lowest-value goods and services identified in a Pareto analysis (Steele and Court, 1996). They are also likely to account for most commodities classified as indirect spend.

Buyer goals for such goods and services should include minimizing the attention paid to the acquisition of such commodities, particularly given the low likely payback that can be expected from such attention or from improvements in procurement in this quadrant (Figure 4.7). Specific tactics may include a systems contract (for example, a corporatewide agreement, often multiyear, with a supplier to purchase a large group of related materials), to leverage the capabilities and inventories of distributors, online ordering, vendor-managed inventory, or other automated purchasing systems (Figure 4.8). A principal challenge for managing orders for these goods and services is to ensure that the purchasing organization can handle the numerous transactions efficiently, without being overwhelmed (Syson, 1992).

Demand for noncritical goods and services can often be easily forecast through analyses of past consumption and order quantities, which, in turn, can help manage purchasing for such items more efficiently. For conglomerates consisting of mostly independent companies or business units and divisions, with each responsible for its own operations (as with the constituent services of DoD) and its own profits and losses, tactics may also include corporate blanket orders enabling users to place repeat orders

Figure 4.4
Different Axis and Quadrant Labels Used for Supply Segmentation Matrixes

Vulnerability		Low value	High value
Buying power (Bristol-Myers Squibb) Degree of supply difficulty (O'Conner) Difficulty of managing purchase (Olsen and Ellram) Number of capable suppliers (Monczka, Trent, and Handfield) Procurement risk (Goldfeld, John Deere) Risk (Savoie; Coyle, Bardi, and Langley) Risk or exposure (Carter) Supply risk (Kraljic) Strategic importance (Owens et al.) Supply market complexity (A.T. Kearney)	High	**Bottleneck** Critical (Carter, O'Conner) Distinctives (Coyle, Bardi, and Langley) Multiple (Monczka, Trent, and Handfield) Strategic security (Steele and Court) Unique products (John Deere) Wheel of fortune (Owens et al.)	**Strategic** Critical items (Savoie) Critical products (John Deere) Criticals (Coyle, Bardi, and Langley) Strategic critical (Steele and Court) Strategic partnership (Owens et al.)
	Low	**Generics** Acquisition (O'Conner; Monczka, Trent, and Handfield; Celestica) Automatic filot (Owens et al.) Efficiency (Bristol-Myers Squibb) Noncritical (A.T. Kearney; Savoie; Coyle, Bardi, and Langley; Goldfeld; Kraljic; Olsen and Ellram) Tactical (Carter) Tactical acquisition (Steele and Court)	**Leverage** Commodities (Coyle, Bardi, and Langley; John Deere) Tactical profit (Steele and Court) The price is tight (Owens et al.)
		Low	High

Value

Business impact (A.T. Kearney)	Profit impact/annual expenditure (O'Conner)
Financial impact (Owens et al.)	Purchase volume (Bristol-Myers Squibb)
Influence on company results (Goldfeld)	Relative cost (Steele and Court)
Profit impact (Kraljic)	Strategic importance of purchase (Olsen and Ellram)

SOURCES: Savoie (2003); A.T. Kearney (2006); Bristol-Meyers Squibb; Carter (1999); O'Conner (2000); Coyle, Bardi, and Langley (2003); Goldfeld (1999); John Deere (1997); Kr
Monczka, Trent, and Handfield (2002); Olsen and Ellram (1997); Owens et al. (1998); Steel and Court (1996).

RAND *MG572-4.4*

Figure 4.5
Goods and Services Linked to Each Quadrant

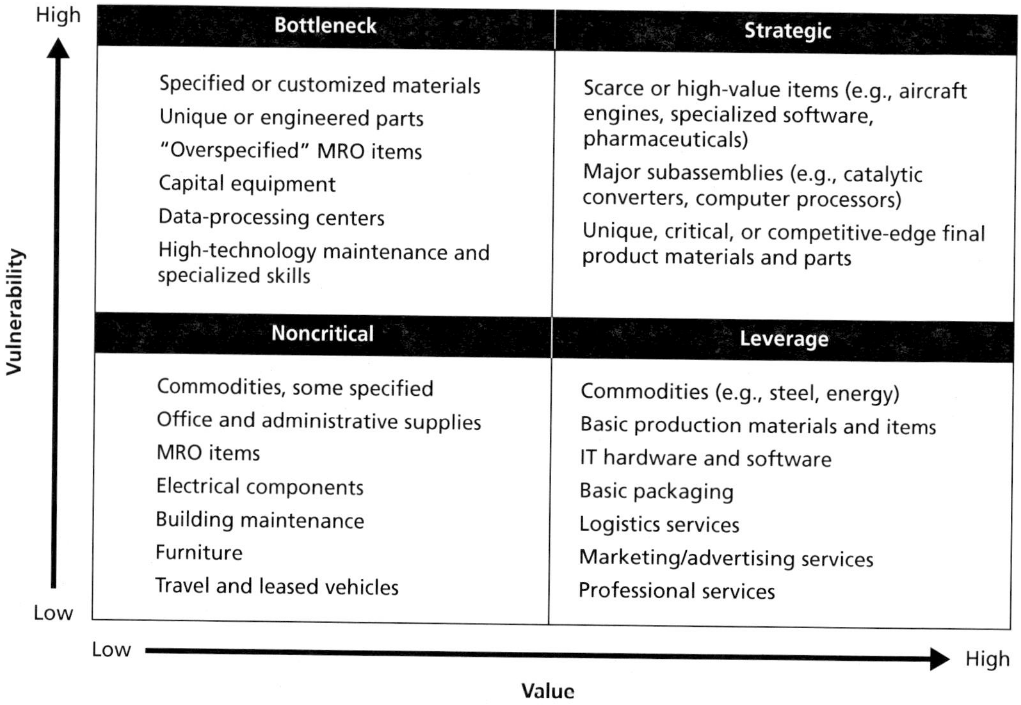

RAND *MG572-4.5*

directly with selected suppliers under previously agreed terms and conditions and to use local suppliers, which may be more responsive.

Leverage. Leverage commodities (high value, low vulnerability) include such goods and services as steel, energy, and other basic production materials and items; standard information technology hardware and software; packaging and logistics services; and marketing and other professional services (Figure 4.5). The market for these goods and services is similar to that for noncritical commodities—highly competitive, with multiple global suppliers offering an abundant supply of easy-to-specify goods and services—albeit with higher costs (Figure 4.6).

Leverage goods and services typically have no availability, quality, safety, reliability, or environmental problems. Buyers can exercise significant power in favorable market conditions for these goods and services (Syson, 1992). Nevertheless, supply development teams should also prepare for less-favorable markets in which prices rise significantly, as they have recently for steel and oil. Short-term contracts can enable buyers to seek lower costs in a flexible market, change suppliers as necessary, and seek new suppliers or new services and products that reduce costs (Steele and Court, 1996).

Figure 4.6
Market Attributes in Each Quadrant

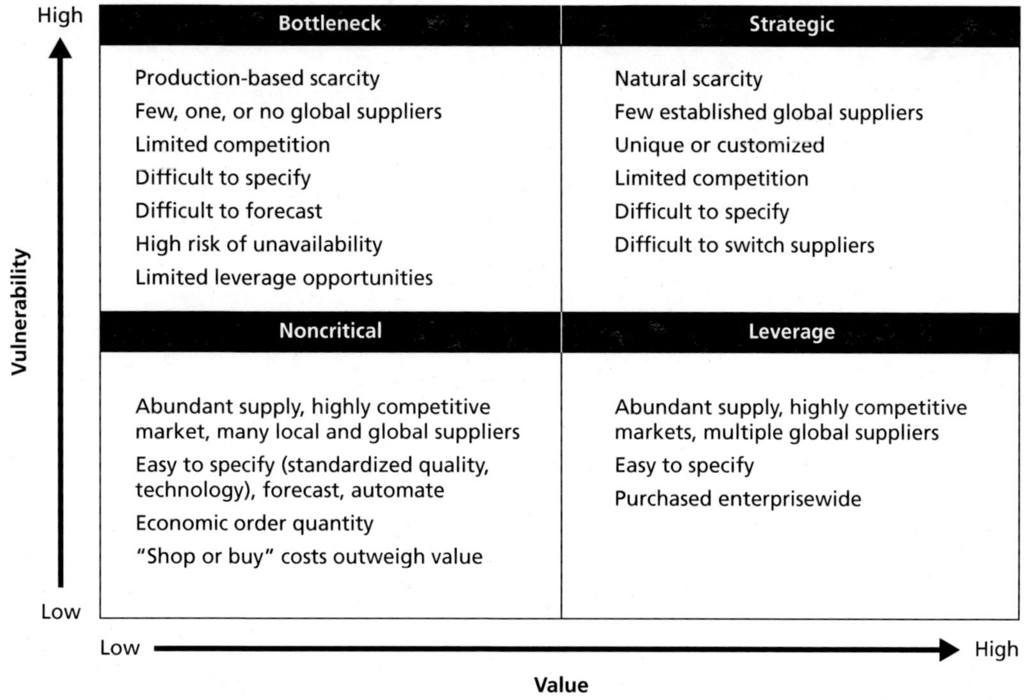

RAND *MG572-4.6*

For easily managed but strategically important goods and services, such as leverage commodities, obtaining a low total cost is critical because the total dollar value of purchases in this category is typically high. Supply management here should see to increase profit margins. Buyers can afford to leverage their buy with a single source with minimal risk to gain volume efficiencies (Figure 4.7). Buyers should also increase their market knowledge to improve the timing of orders (for example, in response to seasonal demand cycles) and become more responsive to market changes (Figure 4.8).

Because there is little to differentiate competing brands of leverage goods and services, suppliers seek to differentiate themselves by their service. Conglomerates may wish to share market information across business units while undertaking separate buying activities because of the difficulties in coordinating a corporatewide response to a rapidly changing market.

Bottleneck. Bottleneck commodities (low value, high vulnerability) include such goods and services as customized materials, unique or engineered parts, nonstandard information technology hardware and software, and technical or other specialized maintenance skills (Figure 4.5). The market for these commodities typically features few global suppliers for goods and services that are difficult to specify and to forecast demand, presenting few leverage opportunities for buying enterprises (Figure 4.6).

Figure 4.7
Buyer Goals and Strategies for Each Quadrant

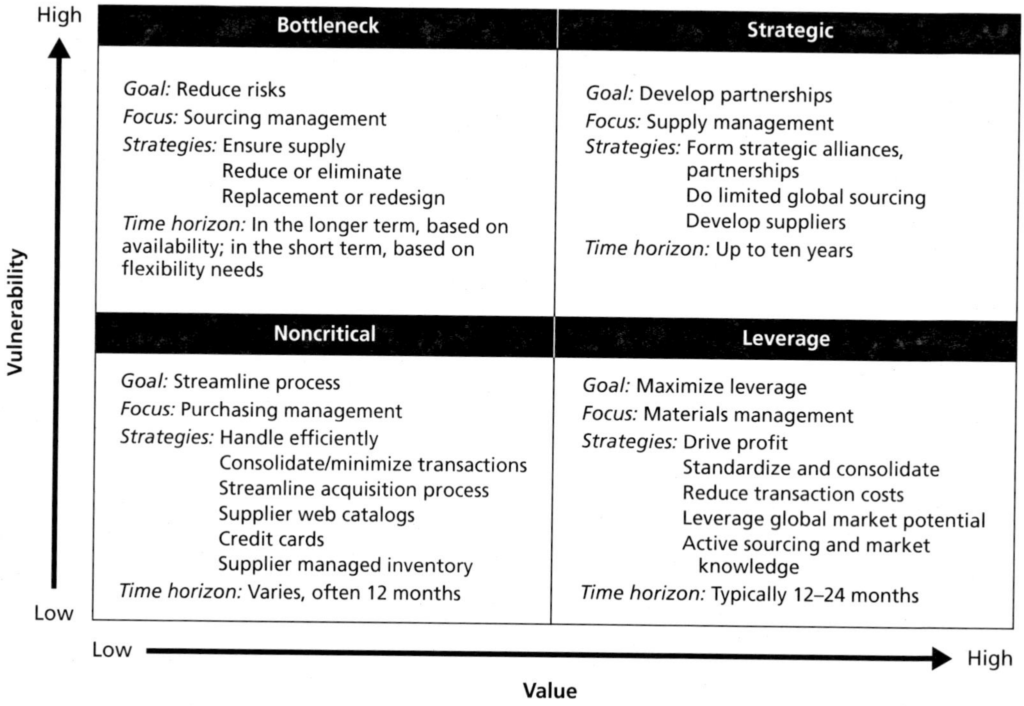

SOURCE: Adapted from Carter (1999).
RAND *MG572-4.7*

Such characteristics make ensuring supply the key buyer goal, perhaps even paying a premium to do so (Figure 4.7). Other buyer strategies might include emphasizing long-term contracts with the use of indices (such as the Producer Price Index) and formulas based on labor and materials to set prices, establishing buffer stocks to achieve security of supply, seeking redesigned or replacement products, or even reducing or eliminating the need for the product (Figure 4.8).

Such goods and services should be reviewed frequently, and their supply markets should be assessed for changes in the supply base and global economy that may affect their availability. For conglomerates, establishing a common catalog for joint safety stock across business units and establishing long-term corporate contracts to increase leverage with suppliers may help reduce the risks associated with bottleneck products.

Strategic. Strategic commodities (high value, high vulnerability) include such goods and services as high-value items (such as aircraft engines, specialized software, pharmaceutical products), major assemblies (such as catalytic converters, computer processors), and other unique, critical products often made in limited amounts but providing a competitive edge to the buyer's final product (Figure 4.5). The market for these valuable goods and services has natural scarcity, with few established global sup-

Figure 4.8
Buyer Tactics in Terms of Key Criteria for Each Quadrant

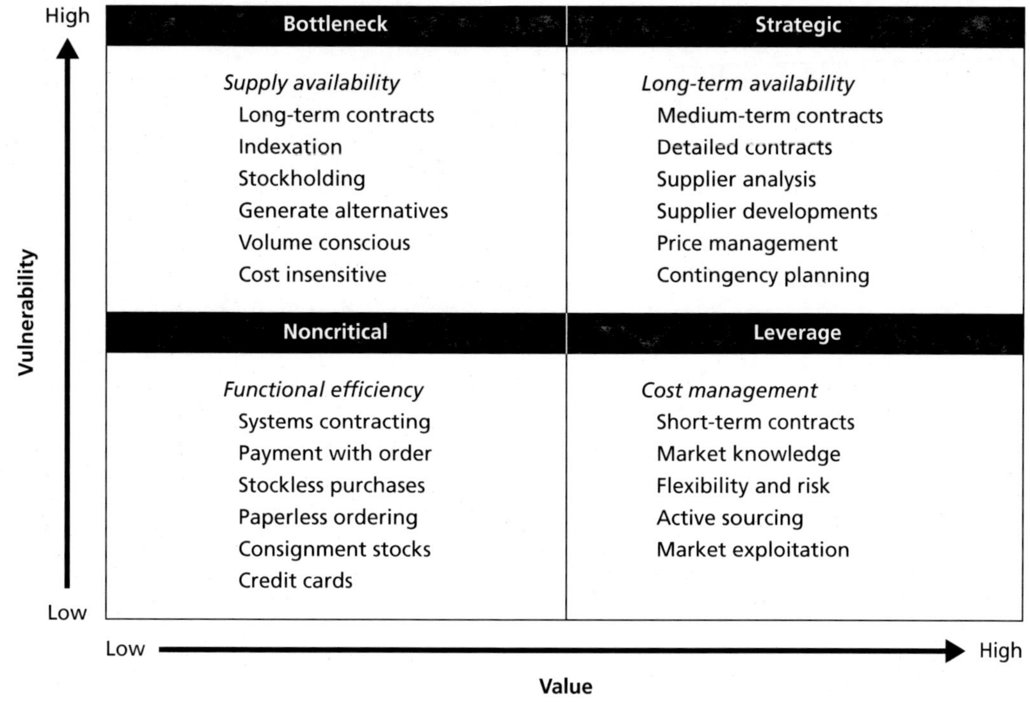

SOURCE: Adapted from Steele and Court (1996).
RAND *MG572-4.8*

pliers for unique or customized commodities that are difficult to specify, and limited competition that makes it difficult to switch suppliers (Figure 4.6). The costs for such goods and services are typically high, and there are significant associated quality, safety, reliability, environmental, or technology issues.

Buyers of these goods and services should seek to manage existing suppliers to ensure current and future availability; monitoring supply and demand, as well as supplier dependencies; and making other efforts to mitigate the lack of competition in the market (Steele and Court, 1996) (Figure 4.7). Specific tactics may include obtaining detailed information on individual suppliers; developing supplier relationships, such as partnerships offering mutual advantage; monitoring and managing price variance; and working closely with suppliers to ensure that they meet production delivery and cost targets and continuously pursue product innovation and development (Figure 4.8).

Because of the high cost and value of strategic commodities, every effort must be made to prevent any potential negative financial effects for the enterprise (Carter, 1999). Given the high vulnerability of these goods and services, it may not be wise to use volume leveraging for them. Conglomerates may wish to manage key suppliers as a group, either through a group purchasing directorate or under the direction of a lead business unit, as well as to seek ways to streamline data gathering, analysis, and decisionmaking. (See Appendix B for more on organizing for supply strategy development.)

Applying Tactics to Quadrants

Supply tactics are not mutually exclusive (Goldfeld, 1999). For example, *cultivating suppliers*—selecting and helping a supplier acquire skills and equipment—can help improve performance for goods and services in the strategic, leverage, and bottleneck quadrants. *Long-term agreements or contracts* can help improve performance for high vulnerability goods and services in the strategic and bottleneck quadrants. *Standardization*—using standard parts and products as much as possible—can improve performance for goods and services in all quadrants. *Price rollbacks*—using quotes from other suppliers to ask preferred suppliers to roll back their prices—can help improve performance for goods and services in leverage and noncritical quadrants, both of which feature abundant supplies in highly competitive markets. *Cross-commodity leveraging*—using suppliers that can provide multiple commodities at competitive prices—can help improve performance for goods and services in leverage, bottleneck, and noncritical quadrants. Some tactics are limited to one quadrant but can still prove effective; for example, using a substitute material or component that is easier to procure than what is currently being purchased can help improve performance for bottleneck goods and services.

To a large degree, the Air Force and DoD already segment spending (Figure 4.9). For example, the General Services Administration (GSA) purchases office supplies and many other goods and services that are common throughout the federal government. These goods and services tend to be generic products of relatively low value and vulnerability. The Defense Logistics Agency (DLA) purchases such commodities as food, clothing, medical supplies, and fuel that tend to be of low vulnerability but of varying value, primarily placing them in both the noncritical and leverage quadrants, with some recent purchases of weapon system consumables in the bottleneck quadrant as well. The Air Force has several organizations, e.g., systems commands, that acquire such goods and services as weapon systems; weapon-system support services; and research, development, testing, and evaluation services. These Air Force commodities have high value and purchasing vulnerability, placing them in the strategic quadrant. Other Air Force organizations, such as the Air Logistics Centers, purchase such goods and services as spare parts and repair for weapon-system sustainment that tend to be in the bottleneck quadrant but can also be in the strategic quadrant. Finally, different Air Force organizations within other major commands purchase such goods and services for base operations support as janitorial and building maintenance services, construction services, and food services that tend to be in the noncritical and leverage quadrants. The personnel skills and levels required for these differing purchasing categories vary considerably, with the lowest skills needed for purchasing noncritical and

Figure 4.9
Notional Placement of Major Air Force Spend Categories in Supply Segmentation Quadrants

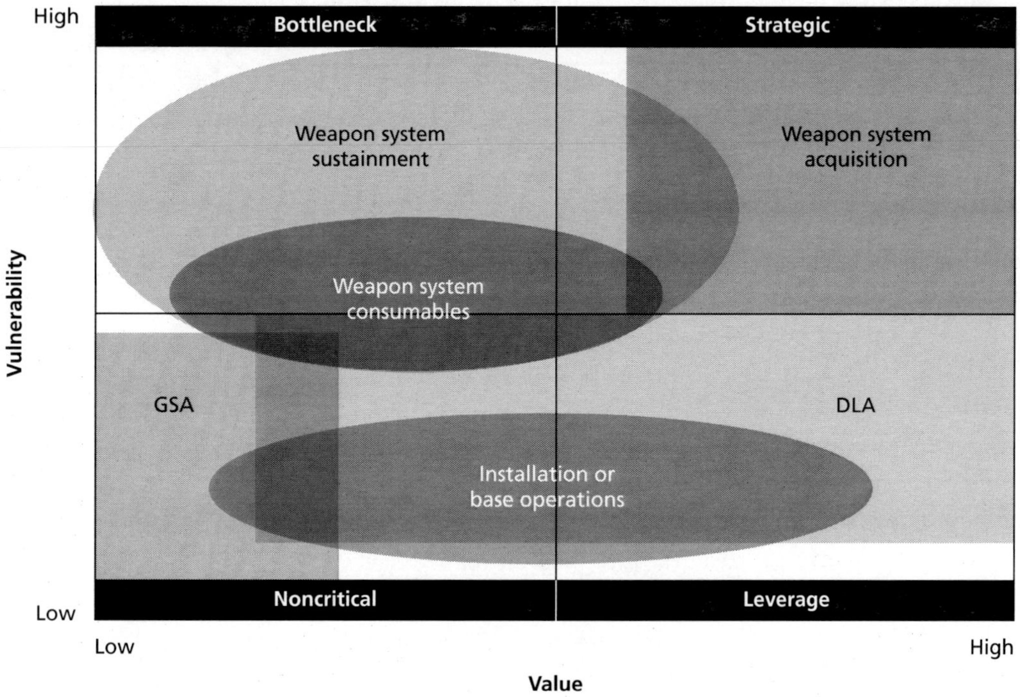

RAND *MG572-4.9*

leverage goods and services, and the highest needed in weapon-system acquisition and other strategic goods and services.[11]

Step 5: Identify and Quantify Prospective Opportunities

Once commodities have been positioned according to their vulnerability and value, buyers can seek to identify and quantify opportunities to improve enterprise operations as well as their prospective business impacts. This can include working through corporate family relationships, interrelated suppliers, and duplicate suppliers while working within the requirements of such special policies as federal mandates for procurement from small and disadvantaged businesses.

Suppliers with multiple contracts, multiple suppliers providing similar products or services, or different agencies purchasing the same goods or services all indicate prospective opportunities for savings through aggregation of requirements to reduce the number of suppliers and contracts. Corporate family relationships, interrelated

[11] For more on personnel skills needed by classification of purchase, see Flynn and Farney (2000) and Raedels (2000).

suppliers, and duplicate suppliers can likewise indicate possibilities for buyers to consolidate and leverage spend. Private-sector firms are significantly reducing the numbers of contracts they have with a single supplier to reduce transaction costs and leverage spend. Cost growth exceeding that of the Producer Price Index may indicate that the supplier is not doing enough to control costs or to identify opportunities for savings.[12] As mentioned earlier, supplier performance data demonstrating varied or poor quality, long or inconsistent wait times, poor information-sharing or supplier innovation, and few multiyear contracts may indicate opportunities for performance improvement.

Markets with few suppliers or limited competition may indicate that suppliers may engage in opportunistic behavior (Williamson, 1985). Past reports, news media, and the DoD Inspector General have documented the fraud and opportunistic behavior of defense contractors, including overcharging or incorrectly billing for work (Pinkham, 2005; Christie, 2005). Suppliers with financial problems also indicate prospective supply risks, particularly from a supplier going out of business or shirking performance.[13] Commodities with low or variable demand indicate that it may be difficult to find and retain good suppliers, particularly given the preferences that many have for stable workloads to minimize operating costs (Hahn, Kim, and Kim, 1986).[14]

The opportunities an enterprise has to realize savings can vary by its current spend and broader market conditions (Hirsch and Barbalho, 2001). An enterprise, as noted earlier, will have greater potential for savings on a commodity for which its spend is large than on those for which its spend is small (Table 2.1). Similarly, a highly fragmented supply base and modest contractual agreements indicate areas for improvement, while strong contractual agreements may indicate that the supply base has already been leveraged. A simple supply market with few suppliers or one at full capacity indicates limited potential for savings, while a complex or competitive supply market indicates greater potential for savings. An enterprise that is not an attractive customer or that suppliers otherwise classify as a nuisance because of its sporadic purchases, unique product specifications, high transaction costs, or limited profit likely has little potential to realize savings, while one suppliers covet for its reputation or regular high-profit purchases has more potential to realize savings. Purchasing enterprises can expect greater savings if individual buyers comply with preferred agreements, while those with lower compliance will typically realize fewer savings. Similarly, an enterprise unwilling to change suppliers has less potential for realizing additional savings than one more willing to do so.

---

[12] See Ellram (2002) or Nelson, Moody, and Stegner (2001) on how John Deere measures cost savings relative to the Producer Price Index.

[13] Dun & Bradstreet, a business information firm, maintains data on profitability, stability, and other operational issues that buyers may use to assess prospective supply risks.

[14] Steele and Court (1996) also notes that uncertainty about the volume of business and future orders (particularly that resulting from short-term contracting and multiple sourcing) gives suppliers few incentives to invest in quality and other improvements or to make other commitments to the buyer.

Table 4.1
Key Factors Affecting Savings Potential in Supply Strategies

	Savings Potential	
	Low	**High**
Volume of spending	Small	Large
Current contractual agreements	Strong	Modest
Complexity of supply market in category	Simple	Complex
Supplier competition in category	Few	Competitive
Attractiveness of company as a customer	Nuisance	Coveted
Ability to specify what the business needs	Generic	Specific
Today's market environment	At full capacity	Eager to deal
Scale of past sourcing efforts	Widespread	Modest
Degree of compliance in using preferred agreements	Limited	Strong
Organization's willingness to change suppliers	Low	High

SOURCE: Adapted from Hirsch and Barbalho, 2001.

Evaluating the expected rewards and risks of prospective PSM initiatives includes identifying expected implementation cost and performance improvements and the timing and required resources for obtaining them. Efforts that require too many resources or too much time to produce results are unlikely to sustain interest and support from senior leadership, particularly for initial PSM efforts.

Step 6: Assess Capabilities and Ease of Internal and External Execution

Enterprises may not at first be able to pursue all prospective opportunities for savings from improved supply strategies (Fawcett, 2000). The degree of effort to develop and execute a specific supply strategy will vary by commodity. Managers must take into account several variables related to the internal and external environments of the corporation as they consider how to add value to their purchasing processes (Fawcett, 2000):

- internal
  - corporate culture
  - personnel readiness and workload
  - competitive priorities
  - functional relationships
  - reward systems

  - data availability
  - socioeconomic goals
- external
  - cultural
  - economic
  - legal
  - political
  - competitive
    - o comparative advantage
    - o core competencies
    - o customer characteristics
    - o industry structure
    - o source and level of competition
    - o supply base capabilities
    - o technology
    - o uncertainty.

Internally, corporate culture, personnel readiness and workload, competitive priorities, functional relationships, reward systems, data availability, preexisting policy goals, and other ongoing initiatives can affect the ability of an enterprise to pursue savings through improved supply strategies. Such variables can affect the ability of an organization to gain visibility into its purchasing practices and implement purchasing strategies to improve these practices. Within the federal government, for example, competition requirements, limitations on contract length, and preferences for purchasing from small business may all affect the options available to purchasing agencies developing supply strategies.[15]

Externally, the competition prevalent in the industry, the effect of the national culture of the enterprise on its place in the global market, and its legal and political circumstances can also affect its opportunities for realizing savings. Competitive factors affecting the ability of an enterprise to realize savings through supply strategies

---

[15] The Competition in Contracting Act requires full and open competition for all federal requirements, which may prevent aggregation of requirements necessary for some PSM initiatives. The Service Contract Act generally limits contract length to five years, which can affect the development of long-term supplier relationships. All federal agencies have a congressional mandate to spend 23 percent of their prime contract dollars for procured goods and services with small businesses, which can affect the size of contracts agencies offer.

Nevertheless, these goals need not preclude all options for PSM initiatives in supply strategies. For example, the Competition in Contracting Act is not applicable when there is only one source for a good or service. Sole-source contracts with a single supplier could therefore perhaps be consolidated without any need to subject the consolidated contract to competition. Previous RAND analyses (such as Moore et al., 2004) have found that relatively few DoD contracts continue for more than one year, much less up to five years. Supply strategies may also seek to foster joint innovations with small businesses and introduce some PSM initiatives relevant to their size (for instance, consolidation of requirements in areas where individual small businesses have many contracts).

include the strength of its core competencies relative to other firms, characteristics of its customers, the structure of its industry, the source and level of its competition, the capabilities of its supply base, the technology of the commodity, and uncertainty in the market. The first-phase assessment of promising areas to implement supply strategies must address both internal and external factors affecting the enterprise.

An infrastructure assessment can enable an enterprise to evaluate its current purchasing practices and capabilities (Smeltzer and Carter, 2001). Such an assessment should include analysis of the enterprise's organizational structure, information technology, and employee capabilities, as well as current purchasing best practices for the commodity. Among infrastructure elements most important for an enterprise seeking to realize savings through improved supply strategies are the following (Smeltzer and Carter, 2001):

- the extent to which purchasing is centralized within the enterprise and that purchasing professionals communicate across different divisions[16]
- the relationship of the chief purchasing officer with the chief executive officer (CEO)[17]
- the qualifications of the purchasing professionals, including their ability to perform rigorous analyses of spending and supply markets and to develop total cost-of-ownership models
- involvement of purchasing professionals with cross-functional commodity teams, which can be key to reducing transaction costs, standardizing purchases, and gaining early supplier involvement
- sophisticated purchasing information technology, important for efforts to reduce transaction costs, purchase prices, and other cost-reduction initiatives, including collaborative design, planning, forecasting, and replenishment.

The degree of effort needed for a successful supply strategy will vary by enterprise and commodity. Among determinants of necessary effort are the complexity of the good or service, the potential for alternative suppliers, the degree of centralization of purchasing within the enterprise, current contractual obligations, resource requirements, and the ability of the enterprise to change suppliers (Sawchuk, 2002).

Enterprises need to consider their capabilities in choosing targets for supply strategies. For example, more resources may be required than an enterprise currently has available to implement a supply strategy. Enterprises may wish to identify targets that have high potentials for improving performance or costs, low vulnerabilities and risks, and can be met with available resources.

---

[16] Centralization can enable leverage buying and development of long-term relationships with suppliers (see Appendix B).

[17] A close relationship can enable CEO support for strategic supplier development efforts.

Step 7: Prioritize Opportunities by Expected Impact and Effort

Once the prospective business benefits (as in step 5) and degree of effort to develop and execute a specific supply strategy for a commodity (as in step 6) have been estimated, the opportunities for cost savings and performance improvements should be prioritized by expected benefit and effort. One means of doing this is plotting each commodity group on a matrix similar to that for supply segmentation, with axes representing business impact and degree of effort required (Sawchuk, 2002; Figure 4.10).

The first, highest priority targets should be the commodity groups requiring the least effort but offering the best results. The next targets should be those that also offer the best results but require more effort. The next groups should be those having less potential, with those requiring less effort preceding those requiring greater effort. In some circumstances, enterprises may also wish, early in their implementation of supply strategies, to address commodities with high numbers of transactions requiring considerable purchasing personnel time or noncritical items whose acquisition could be automated, thereby freeing the time of these personnel to address more-complex commodity groupings.

Figure 4.10
Prioritizing Opportunities by Expected Impact and Effort

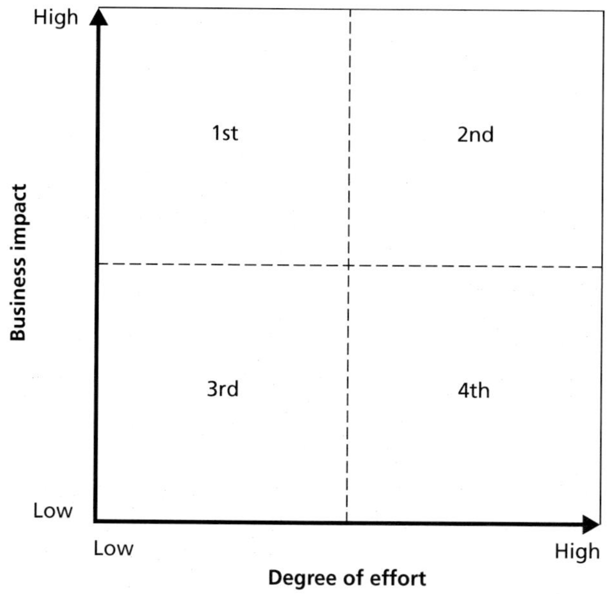

SOURCE: Adapted from Sawchuk (2002).
NOTE: Begin in upper left (first) quadrant.
RAND *MG572-4.10*

The steps outlined above can suffice for a general, high-level overview to identify broad areas of spend across an enterprise to prioritize and target PSM initiatives within it, based on where the greatest results can be expected. In Chapter Five, we outline a second phase for developing and executing initiatives for individual commodities or groupings as identified in the above steps. The second phase requires both greater overall and more-detailed effort on individual initiatives, in turn requiring a higher degree of rigorous analysis.

CHAPTER FIVE

Developing a Supply Strategy: Developing and Executing a Commodity Group Strategy

Once all commodities have been grouped, segmented, and prioritized, the enterprise is ready to develop and execute tailored supply strategies for the commodity groups that will produce the best results and that require the least effort for the greatest return. Steps for doing this (as shown earlier as the last six steps in phase II) include

- assigning and providing resources for cross-functional teams to develop supply strategies for commodity groups selected in phase I
- developing a more-detailed and analytically rigorous profile of the selected commodity groups
- analyzing the industry or its supply market
- identifying and prioritizing risks and vulnerabilities in the market
- developing the strategy for each group
- executing the strategy.

Many of these steps parallel those in phase I but are more detailed and are applied in a more analytically rigorous way to specific commodities rather than to the entire spend of an enterprise. These steps, which we review below, also parallel many strategic sourcing processes in the literature.[1] Just as enterprise goals and objectives should guide the supply grouping, positioning, segmentation, and prioritization of phase I, they

---

1 For example, Strategic Sourcing Initiative teams at Gillette employ a formal seven-step strategic sourcing process methodology for competitive sourcing and to evaluate suppliers on cost, quality, and services provided (see, among others, Dolan and Fedele, 2004). The steps of this process, developed with the management consulting firm A. T. Kearney, include the following:

1. Develop category profile.
2. Generate supplier portfolio.
3. Develop sourcing strategy.
4. Select implementation path.
5. Negotiate and select suppliers.
6. Implement agreements.
7. Continuous improvement.

should also guide the supply strategy development of phase II. Phase II analysis can help identify not just the parameters of the relationship between a buyer and a supplier for a given item in the supply chain but also the position of a commodity or group of commodities within a supply network, including how the availability of the commodity affects other network activities (Dubois and Pedersen, 2002).

Step 8: Assign and Resource a Cross-Functional Team to Each Commodity Initiative

The first step in launching specific commodity initiatives for developing and executing supply strategies is to assign and provide resources for cross-functional teams assigned to each commodity group. Such teams are often called *commodity councils.*[2]

These councils parallel the cross-functional teams of step 1, which were assigned to group, segment, and prioritize all spend across the enterprise. In this case, representatives from such functions as purchasing, engineering, manufacturing, customer support, supplier relations, logistics, finance, quality control, and legal affairs assemble to develop a tailored supply strategy for each of the most promising commodity groups identified in the first phase. Because they examine specific commodity groups in depth, council members should have backgrounds and analytic skills that focused more on the selected commodity and therefore should be better able to analyze it more rigorously.

Including members from varying corporate functions here will help ensure support across the corporation for the supply strategy the council develops and will also lead to more rigorous examinations of current and future requirements, supply base capabilities, and purchasing decisions. Not all members may participate equally over time. Some will work full time on commodity supply strategies; some will do so part time; and some will do so as occasionally needed.

Homogeneous enterprises—especially those that find it easier to centralize purchases for goods and services—will typically house their commodity councils in corporate headquarters. Conglomerates—especially those comprising multiple strategic business units (SBUs) with different products and missions—may wish to house the commodity councils for more-strategic goods and services in business units for which the commodity is most important (Goldfeld, 1999). Within DoD, for example, the Army, Navy, and Air Force all purchase jet engines, but the Air Force buys far more than any other service. Efforts to develop a DoD-wide supply strategy for jet engines might therefore be centralized within the Air Force but could also include representa-

---

[2] The name of this team can vary; some firms call it a *purchasing team*; some call it a *commodity team*; and some call it a *commodity council*. We use the last of these because this is the name that similar teams within the Air Force carry. Air Force commodity councils are permanent, cross-functional teams that serve as mechanisms for efficiently implementing strategic sourcing (Williams, 2005).

tives from the Army, Navy, and Marine Corps. For more common commodities, such as facilities support services, personal computers and their software, office supplies, and travel services, the single largest user is less important. Centralization within DoD of supplier relationships and supply strategy development can help provide purchasing leverage across DoD.[3]

In addition to varying by type of enterprise, the right balance between centralized and decentralized control can also vary by commodity (Laseter, 1998). Commodities and their councils may be centrally controlled and managed for the benefit of the enterprise as a whole, centrally led to ensure corporate coverage (and consistent policies, practices, and processes among SBUs) but with ownership by the business units that are the key buyers, or controlled by business units that develop strategies independently. From an enterprise perspective, the proper model for management and control often depends on the uniqueness or commonality of requirements, the complexity of modeling processes, and the locus of corporate leverage. From a business unit perspective, it may depend on the importance of the commodity to production or to the final product, as well as on issues of integrating design and logistics. Other criteria for selecting the proper model of management and control include the locus of technical or engineering knowledge, design and production, purchasing skills, knowledge of the commodity and its market, and strengths of supplier relationships by business unit.

Step 9: Develop a More-Detailed Profile of the Selected Commodity Groups

The commodity council, once assembled, builds on the phase I analyses and develops a more-detailed profile of its chosen commodity group. This includes past, present, and future user requirements and priorities for it (both across the enterprise and at individual locations), what affects demand for it, order quantities and patterns, spend for it, what affects prices and total costs for it, specifications, current performance of the supply base, and initial assessment of opportunities for a supply strategy.

The first step in developing this profile is commodity research analysis, defining the requirements of the enterprise or a specific business unit for the commodity, which are derived from their strategies (Monczka, Trent, and Handfield, 2002). This also includes assessing past and current spend on the commodity group and individual items within it and by its suppliers, characteristics of the supply market, and current and projected requirements. The initial opportunity assessment that results from profiling the commodity can be based on analysis of such key factors as the number of contracts per supplier, the number of suppliers per major commodity, and the current performance of suppliers (Eversbusch, 1998). The commodity council should begin

---

3 Appendix B describes how to determine where to place purchasing organizations within an enterprise.

by verifying that the spend requirements have been grouped in the right way, that is, whether other goods and services should be added to or subtracted from the grouping under consideration or whether the grouping should be divided into smaller groups.[4]

An effective profile must reflect a solid understanding of all major factors affecting cost and quality and of the flexibility in addressing them (Laseter, 1998). The requirements analysis for the commodity profile should also include an understanding of the tolerance of risk for the commodity (Zsidisin, Ragatz, and Melnyk, 2003).

One way to understand the cost, quality, and risks of producing a commodity is to map the production process, documenting practice and technology options at each stage and building up costs by each step of the process (Laseter, 1998). While strategy development generally requires high-level cost models based on an understanding of such major cost factors as raw materials, labor, technology, volume, and set-up time, supplier selection requires even more-detailed, comparative cost models tailored to specific suppliers.

One way to consider the cost of a good or service in the purchaser's manufacturing process is examining the components of total procurement cost (Coyle, Bardi, and Langley, 2003). The most obvious component of the total procurement cost is the basic input cost—the price—but other components include detecting the need or requirement; ordering, creating, and managing a supplier relationship; transportation; quality control; and receiving and making the commodity ready for use. Value can be added to a purchase by reducing any of these costs.

Step 10: Analyze the Industry and the Supply Market for a Specific Commodity Group

Once the commodity team develops a detailed profile of the good or service it is examining, it should analyze the industry and supply market for it. This includes determining how the commodity fits into the value stream of the enterprise (the activities of the enterprise to design, order, and provide a specific good or service); determining supplier costs, capabilities, portfolios, and strategies; assessing the structure of the industry; and determining the relative power of the buyer and supplier. Developing an industry map—a one-page diagram of the supply industry highlighting the flow of products—can be a good place to begin (see Laseter, 1998, for an example of an industry map).

Industry Structure

Michael Porter has described techniques for analyzing industries and competitors and for creating and sustaining superior performance (Porter, 1975, 1980, and 1985). He identified five competitive forces that determine industry competitiveness and struc-

---

[4] See Appendix A for more on grouping requirements for supply strategies.

ture: the threat of new entrants, the threat of substitute products or services, the bargaining power of customers, the bargaining power of suppliers, and rivalry among existing firms (Figure 5.1). Porter emphasizes that industry dynamics go beyond the rivalry among existing firms, as represented by the curved arrow in the center box (the current industry), and must also include how buyers, suppliers, substitute products, and potential entrants can affect the industry. The resulting five forces influence the prices, costs, and required investments of firms in an industry. The strength of each of these five forces is a function of the underlying economic and technical characteristics of an industry. Almost universally, companies and consulting firms use Porter's "five forces" model to analyze industry structure and competition.

Porter's research (1975, 1985) indicates that potential new entrants to an industry can face *market entry barriers*, such as those the following can pose:

- *Economies of scale.* The market for express delivery of packages is an example of this. New competitors would face enormous costs to replicate the systems that Federal Express, United Parcel Service, or DHL Worldwide Express already have in place.
- *Proprietary product differences.* Markets for proprietary products are limited precisely by the nature of the product.
- *Strong brand identities.*

Figure 5.1
Elements of Industry Structure

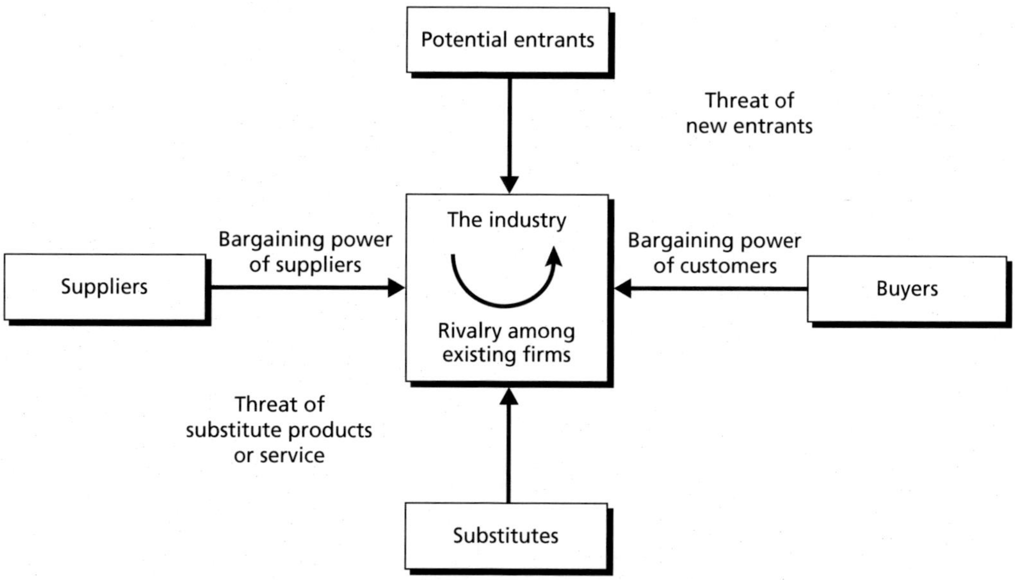

SOURCE: Porter (1975). Used with permission.
RAND *MG572-5.1*

- *High buyer switching costs.* If a buyer is highly integrated with a supplier, it may appear too costly to switch to a new supplier.
- *High, fixed entry costs or capital improvements.*
- *Absolute cost advantages reflected in proprietary learning curves or access to the necessary inputs or proprietary low-cost product designs of competitors.*
- *Government policy limiting the market.* Government policies can limit markets; for example, foreign government policies prevent U.S. firms from entering some foreign markets.
- *Expected retaliation.* A firm entering a new market may, for example, face retaliatory competition in other markets from competitors in the new markets it has entered.

The following are some of the determinants of Porter's competitive forces:

- rivalry among existing firms and the threat of new entrants, including
  - slow industry growth
  - high fixed or storage costs and value added
  - intermittent overcapacity
  - product differences
  - brand identity
  - switching costs
  - concentration and balance within the industry
  - informational complexity
  - diversity of competitors
  - corporate stakes
  - exit barriers
- the threat of substitute products or service, including
  - price of substitutes
  - switching costs
  - buyer propensity to adopt substitutes
- the bargaining power of suppliers, including
  - technological stability
  - switching costs
  - presence of substitutes
  - supplier concentration
  - market size and capacity
- the bargaining power of customers, including
  - such bargaining leverage variables as buyer and supplier concentration (for example, buyer volume compared to supply capacity, growth in demand relative to capacity switching costs, ability to backward integrate [to produce the commodity internally], and substitution possibilities)

- such price sensitivity variables as total purchases, product differences, brand identity, relationship between price and quality, and decisionmakers' incentives.

Given a particular industry structure, suppliers will be attracted to a customer principally by profitability but may also be attracted by opportunities to grow, associate with an industry leader, acquire technical or other knowledge, and receive prompt payment. Competitive positioning for suppliers includes assessing their ability to compete for business on the basis of costs, technical advantage, superior logistics, a highly supportive marketing network, or some other edge.

Porter suggests beginning an industry analysis with a general overview, including determining who is in the industry, locating and reviewing industry studies, and consulting annual reports of publicly held companies. He cautions against spending too much time on published sources with limited timeliness, aggregation, and depth. Instead, he recommends getting into the field as early as possible and gathering published material and conducting field interviews simultaneously, which he believes to be more efficient.[5]

For raw data in an industry analysis, Porter (1980) recommends including information on

- product lines
- buyers and their behavior
- complementary products
- substitute products
- growth, including rate, pattern (seasonal, cyclical), and determinants
- technology of production and distribution, including cost structure, economies of scale, value added, logistics, and labor
- marketing and selling, including market segmentation and marketing practices
- suppliers
- distribution channels (if indirect)
- innovation, including types, sources, rate, and economies of scale
- competitors, including strategy, goals, strengths and weaknesses, and assumptions
- social, political, and legal environments
- macroeconomic environment.

These data should be compiled by company, year, and functional area.

[5] For a more thorough discussion of industry structure and conducting an industry analysis, see Porter (1980, especially Chapter 1 and Appendix B).

For field data, Porter suggests gathering information on

- suppliers
- distributors
- customers
- service organizations
  - trade associations
  - investment banks
  - consultants
  - auditors
  - commercial banks
  - advertising agencies
- industry observers
  - standard setting organizations (such as Underwriters Laboratory)
  - unions
  - press, particularly editors of trade press and local press where competitors' facilities or headquarters are located
  - local organizations (such as the Chamber of Commerce) where facilities or headquarters are located
  - state government
  - federal government
  - international organizations (such as the Organisation for Economic Co-operation and Development and the United Nations)
  - watchdog groups (such as Consumer's Union)
  - financial community (securities analysts)
  - agencies involved in regulation, industry promotion, and financing
- sources inside the company that are knowledgeable about competitors
  - market research staff
  - sales force
  - service organizations
  - former employees or competitors, observers, or service organizations
  - engineering staff
  - purchasing department and its contact with suppliers that call on competitors
  - research and development department, which generally follows technical developments and scientific conferences and publications.

For more details on market research, see Nicosia and Moore (2006).

Supplier Segmentation of Buyers

In recent years, sophisticated sales organizations have moved away from traditional promotion of volume sales regardless of profit to a system of key account management.

In this system, suppliers assess the true cost—including, for example, overhead for each customer and special buyer demands—and thereby the profitability and attractiveness of doing business with each customer for each good or service.[6] Suppliers use this information to develop strategies for their customers, just as buyers develop strategies for interacting with their suppliers.

One way that suppliers segment their customers is by the relative *value* of the buyer's business, including the profits that can be realized in the goods and services a customer purchases, and the *attractiveness* of the account, including the reputation or name recognition of a buyer (Figure 5.2). Suppliers may show little interest in and offer little support to *nuisance customers* (low value, low attractiveness) and may even actively seek to withdraw from the customer or industry because doing so would have few or no adverse effects. They may seek to derive maximum short-term benefit from *exploitable customers* (high value, low attractiveness, perhaps because of unfavorable operating conditions) without concern about losing them; one way is a steep price increase. They may want to work hard, at least in the short term, to meet or exceed the requirements of *development customers* (low value, high attractiveness) to win more business. Finally, they may seek strategic alliances and other ways of locking in *core customers* (high value and high attractiveness).

Figure 5.2
Notional Supplier Assessment of Customers

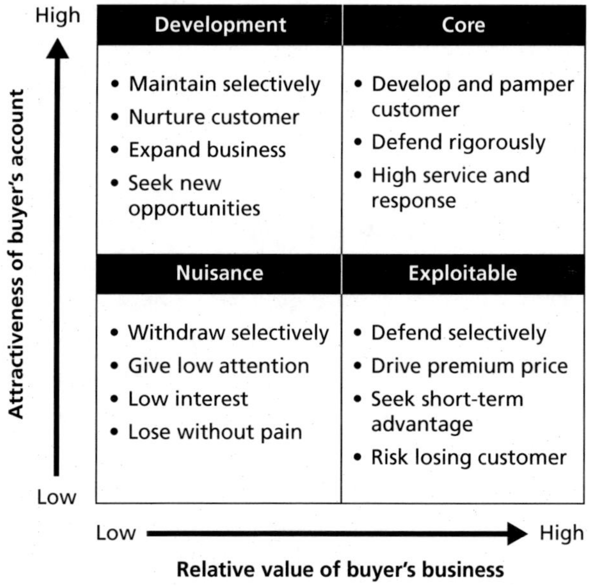

SOURCE: Adapted from Steele and Court (1996).
RAND *MG572-5.2*

6 This discussion is based largely on Steele and Court (1996).

Buyer Responses to Supplier Segmentation

Because suppliers segment their markets, purchasers need to determine, as well as possible, how suppliers perceive their business (Steele and Court, 1996). This effort should include coordinated multifunctional activities, such as discussions with and visits to suppliers. Comparing how buyers and sellers position each other in the terms we have been discussing can suggest whether the appropriate supplier and strategy have been selected and what synergies and other considerations might exist.

Suppliers are unlikely to reveal their exact strategies to buyers, but a buyer may be able to discern broad indicators (such as technology, price) that will help it determine whether a supplier is a good match for it.

Buyer and Supplier Power

Another way to consider the relationship between buyer and supplier and its implications for a specific commodity group is by assessing the power of the buyer relative to that of the supplier compared to the power of the supplier relative to that of the buyer.[7] *Buyer dominance*, which features high buyer power but relatively low supplier power (such as the power Wal-Mart exercises in many industries), allows the buyer to seek greater leverage on quality and cost, gaining above-normal returns but giving up only normal returns to the supplier. *Interdependence*, in which both buyer and supplier have high power and significant leverage opportunities, requires the two parties to work closely together; for example, the supplier may achieve above-normal returns but also pass some value to the buyer in the form of greater returns or increased innovation. *Independence*, in which neither the buyer nor the supplier has significant power or leverage opportunities, requires both to accept the current prevailing price and quality levels. *Supplier dominance*, which features high supplier power and low buyer power, allows the supplier to exploit its relationship with the buyer, getting above-normal returns on the good or service.

Buyers can choose several ways to improve their power relative to suppliers. To move away from supplier dominance or interdependence toward independence or buyer dominance, buyers may, among other tactics, increase their share of the market, increase the number of suppliers in the market, increase the dependency of suppliers on the buyer, or seek standardization of supply. In response, suppliers may pursue countervailing strategies by providing value-added activities that make their products more nearly unique or acquire other, similar suppliers to reduce the supply base. In sum, the relative powers of buyers and suppliers can vary and occasionally prevent buyers from accomplishing what they would like in a supplier relationship.

In assessing the supply market, buyers should do the following (Monczka, Trent, and Handfield, 2002):

---

[7] This discussion is based largely on Cox (2001).

- Identify current and potential suppliers.
- Define the marketplace by identifying best and average price.
- Determine expected pricing trends.
- Identify the strategies of market leaders.
- Determine information technology requirements.
- Determine current and future volume requirements by location.
- Seek opportunities to leverage expenditures on the commodity with those for similar commodities.

Supplier literature, government reports, trade magazines, and other database searches, as well as benchmarking data gathered through interviews with suppliers and their customers, will provide the information for assessing supply markets (Nicosia and Moore, 2006).

No list of evaluation criteria is equally applicable to every buyer in every industry (Kraljic, 1983). Furthermore, the relative importance of different criteria can vary with technological changes or shifts in competitive dynamics. If, for example, a particular good or service is labor-intensive, understanding labor rates is necessary for understanding the market for it. If a good uses titanium, understanding the titanium supply industry and prices is essential to understanding its market.

Step 11: Identify and Prioritize Prospective Risks and Vulnerabilities

Supply failure, poor or highly variable quality, high costs, and slow delivery risks have always existed. Traditionally, enterprises have sought to "buffer" such risks through multiple suppliers, extensive competition, expediting, larger order quantities, and safety stocks (Giunipero and Eltantawy, 2004). Nevertheless, such buffering strategies have also had associated risks and costs, such as long lead times, inconsistent or highly variable supplies, and too much or the wrong inventory.

Many newer purchasing and supply-chain management practices (such as outsourcing, supply base rationalization, and lean inventories) and the increasing pace of industry consolidations and technological changes have reduced some risks but have increased others and also added new ones (Zsidisin, Panelli, and Upton, 2000). In general, these changes have increased the "brittleness" of supply chains and the exposure of an enterprise to supply disruptions. They have also thereby increased the importance of shifting from reactive supply risk buffering to proactive understanding and effective management of supply risks and vulnerabilities (Zsidisin, Ragatz, and Melnyk, 2003).

Consequently, after analyzing the industry and supply market for its commodity group, the commodity council should identify prospective risks and vulnerabilities that could affect supply, determine their probability, and assess their likely effects, including their scale, duration, and required recovery costs. Once it has identified the prospective risks, the commodity council should prioritize and develop ways to prevent, mitigate, or manage them, such as through contingency action plans (Steele and Court, 1996; Christopher, 2003; Zsidisin, Ragats, and Melnyk, 2005). Events affecting supply may include supplier failure, natural disasters, bombings or terrorist attacks, cartel actions or strikes, and sudden increases in demand that can constrain the capacity of the supply chain.

In the view of some analysts (for example, Steele and Court, 1996), the prime task of an effective purchasing organization is to secure supply regardless of broader forces in the purchasing environment. Risk management for such organizations comprises examining the entire upstream supply chain for a good or service to identify future supply problems.

Risks vary by commodity, product, or service, and identifying, assessing, and planning for them requires considerable personnel time and resources (Giunipero and Eltantawy, 2004). It is therefore often best to start by focusing on strategic or bottleneck goods and services and then on leverage commodities (Steele and Court, 1996).[8] While developing additional sources of supply can help reduce risks, having such approved sources does not necessarily reduce vulnerabilities. Existing suppliers might be able to offer options for reducing vulnerabilities. One way would be for the supplier to offer a second manufacturing plant to serve as a backup for the first in case of disaster. Buyers should ensure that their suppliers have plans to address a wide variety of contingencies.[9]

While there is an abundance of literature on risk, research on supply risk assessments, contingency plans, and management is limited (Zsidisin, Panelli, and Upton, 2000). Nevertheless, a number of methodologies have been proposed for these tasks. Below we outline a composite process for risk assessment and management.

The first step is to recognize that supply vulnerabilities exist (Zsidisin, Ragatz, and Melnyk, 2003). The commodity council needs to be aware that its actions or lack of action creates various supply risks.

The second step is to identify prospective supply vulnerabilities. The commodity council should identify all prospective risks associated with a proposed supply strategy. Risks may be identified through "brainstorming," interviews, workshops, supply-

---

8 Giunipero and Eltantawy (2004) notes that companies must balance the benefits gained through risk management and the cost incurred by these practices. They discuss four situational buying factors—degree of product technology, need for security, importance of the supplier, and prior experience of purchasers—that are critical to determining the level of resources needed for risk management.

9 To reduce single-source risk to its just-in-time processes, Honda of America requires its suppliers to have dual capability (Nelson, Mayo, and Moody, 1998). For more on supply vulnerability and competitive advantage, see Sheffi (2005) and Sheffi and Rice (2005).

chain mapping or other form of description, the Delphi method,[10] fault or event tree analysis,[11] or nominal group techniques[12] (Ziegenbein and Nienhaus, 2004; Zsidisin, Panelli, and Upton, 2000). Some authors recommend assessing vulnerabilities by categories of external risks, such as demand, supply, and environment, and internal risks, such as control, process, and contingency (Peck et al., 2003).[13] Others recommend a less structured approach so as not to inhibit creative thinking (Steele and Court, 1996).

After identifying the vulnerabilities, the commodity council should estimate their likelihood. Some authors (such as Steele and Court, 1996) recommend assigning a relative weight (for example, *high*, *medium*, or *low*) to their probability of occurrence, while others (e.g., Ziegenbein and Nienhaus, 2004) recommend differing classifications (for example, *unlikely*, *possible*, *likely*, and *very likely*).

The commodity council next needs to assess the relative consequences or significance of a prospective loss. The consequences of a given risk are a function of its scale, scope, duration, recovery time, and total cost (Steele and Court, 1996). These possible consequences can be ranked as low or high (Steele and Court, 1996) or as low, medium, significant, and threat to existence (Ziegenbein and Nienhaus, 2004).

---

[10] Linstone and Turoff (2002, pp. 1 and 3) describes the Delphi method:

> Delphi may be characterized as a method for structuring a group communication process so that the process is effective in allowing a group of individuals, as a whole, to deal with a complex problem . . . . Usually Delphi undergoes four distinct phases. The first phase is characterized by exploration of the subject under discussion, wherein each individual contributes additional information he feels is pertinent to the issue. The second phase involves the process of reaching an understanding of how the group views the issue (i.e., where the members agree or disagree and what they mean by relative terms such as importance, desirability, or feasibility). If there is significant disagreement, then that disagreement is explored in the third phase to bring out the underlying reasons for the differences and possibly to evaluate them. The last phase, a final evaluation, occurs when all previously gathered information has been initially analyzed and the evaluations have been fed back for consideration.

[11] Schellhorn, Thums, and Reif (2002, esp. p. 1) notes that fault or event tree analysis breaks down a system risk event into component failures step by step by linking failure events with their causes. Because fault tree analysis is used for qualitative and quantitative analysis of systems, it is essential that the fault tree include every cause for a risk and, conversely, that every cause is actually needed to trigger the event.

[12] Van De Ven and Delbecq (1974, p. 606) defines the *nominal group technique* as

> a group meeting in which a structured format is utilized for decision making among individuals seated at a table. This structured format proceeds as follows: (a) Individual members first silently and independently generate their ideas on a problem or task in writing. (b) This period of silent writing is followed by a recorded round-robin procedure in which each group member (one at a time, in turn, around the table) presents one of his ideas to the group without discussion. The ideas are summarized in a terse phrase and written on a blackboard or sheet of paper on the wall. (c) After all individuals have presented their ideas, there is a discussion of the recorded ideas for the purposes of clarification and evaluation. (d) The meeting concludes with a silent voting on priorities by individuals through a rank ordering or rating procedure, depending upon the group's decision rule. The "group decision" is the pooled outcome of individual votes.

[13] Appendix C outlines more prospective risks.

Because it would be prohibitively expensive to eliminate all supply risks, the commodity council should prioritize them according to their significance and should focus risk-mitigation efforts on those most threatening to the enterprise. The council may wish to plot risks according to their probabilities of occurrence and expected consequences, determining an "acceptable" risk frontier (Figure 5.3).

For low-priority risks (low probability, low impact), the commodity council may wish to accept the risk rather than expend resources to address it. For high-priority risks, the council may seek to avoid or reduce the likelihood of the risk. If this is not possible, the council needs to identify prospective measures for mitigating the risk (Ziegenbein and Nienhaus, 2004). Prospective actions may vary by effectiveness, duration, and probability of the risk and range from eliminating the need that produces the risk to finding alternatives for the commodity to taking no immediate action (Table 5.1). Because some prospective risk-prevention or mitigation efforts can be quite costly, the commodity council needs to evaluate the costs and benefits of each prospective strategy. It should then gain management support and implement the strategies that are cost effective (Kiser and Cantrell, 2006).

Not all risks may be avoided at a reasonable cost. Hence, the commodity council should also develop contingency plans, which are detailed recovery and remediation plans for shortening the duration of a prospective disruption resulting from a risk,

Figure 5.3
Understanding Risk Exposure

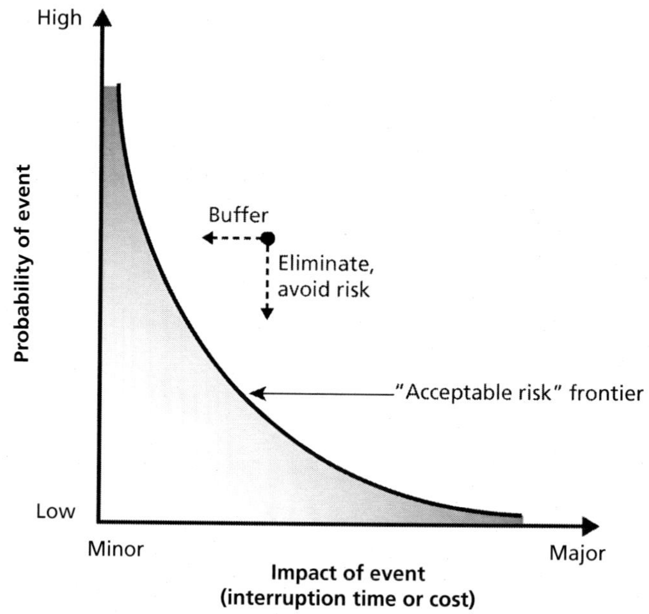

SOURCE: Zsidisin, Ragatz, and Melnyk (2003). Used with permission.
RAND *MG572-5.3*

Table 5.1
Prospective Actions to Mitigate Risks and Vulnerabilities

Priority	Probability	Duration	Impact	Prospective Actions
1	High	Long	High	Structure contingency plan Invest to eliminate need Find possible alternatives
2	Medium	Long	High	Structure contingency plan Invest to eliminate need Find possible alternatives
3	High	Short	High	Act to minimize impact Accept high-cost options? Consider extra inventory
4	Medium	Short	High	Pay to minimize impact? Accept high-cost options?
5	High	Long	Low	Pay to eliminate? Find alternatives
6	Low	Long	High	Pay to minimize effects? Consider alternatives
7	Medium	Long	Low	Accept high-cost options? Pay to minimize duration?
8	Low	Short	High	Accept high-cost options?
9	Low	Long	Low	Accept high-cost options?
10	High	Short	Low	No immediate action
11	Medium	Short	Low	No immediate action
12	Low	Short	Low	No immediate action

SOURCE: Steele and Court (1996).

minimizing its consequences, and identifying the resources necessary to execute the plans (Zsidisin, Ragatz, and Melnyk, 2003).

Finally, risk assessment and management require continuous learning and knowledge management. Thus, when a supply disruption occurs, a commodity council needs to conduct post-incident audits to determine the root cause of the disruption and document any lessons learned to improve management of similar future events. The audits should also address any deficiencies identified in past risk assessments, mitigation strategies, and contingency plans (Zsidisin, Ragatz, and Melnyk, 2003).

Supplier participation is necessary for a vulnerability analysis (Steele and Court, 1996). Solutions must be kept as simple as possible because few organizations have the resources needed to eliminate all vulnerabilities.

Step 12: Develop a Strategy

Once the commodity council has developed a more-detailed profile of its selected good or service, analyzed the industry and supply market for it, and identified and prioritized prospective risks and vulnerabilities and responses to them, it is ready to develop a supply strategy. Below we review supply strategy components, defining supplier roles within them, tailoring tactics to commodity categories (including how buyers may respond to supplier tactics in differing categories of commodities), planning evaluations, and documenting strategy.

Supply Strategy Components

Supply strategies can vary by *buying policy*, *number of sources*, *type of source*, and *length of the relationship*.[14] Among the range of buying policies a firm may pursue are

- subsistence—reactive or tactical strategies for purchases to meet immediate requirements
- forward—planning or anticipating purchases to secure lower prices through quantity discounts or lower transportation costs
- speculative—buying beyond current or expected needs in anticipation of a price increase or supply shortage
- volume purchase—agreements stipulating the total volume to be purchased over time
- life-of-product—awarding business for future demand to a supplier to ensure future availability of the good or service
- consignment—allowing the enterprise to stock the items at its own location before making the purchase, with the supplier not charging the enterprise until it is actually used.

The number of sources will vary according to whether the source is *sole* (only one source is available), *single* (buyers choose to use only one source to increase leverage or for other advantages), or *multiple*.

Buyers must consider several issues to determine the right type of source for their needs. For example, buyers may need to consider whether to have directed sourcing policies specifying particular suppliers; to purchase directly from manufacturers offering volume discounts or from distributors offering favorable terms for smaller purchases; or to pursue, in association with other buyers, cooperative or leveraged buying, joint ventures, or integrated supply in association with other buyers to increase purchasing effectiveness, achieve economies of scale, or spread risk and expense.

---

[14] This discussion is based largely on Raedels (2000) and Dobler and Burt (1996).

The length of the supply relationship will vary according to the volatility of supply markets, industry practices, and the needs of the buying enterprise. According to Anderson and Jap (2005, pp. 78–79),

> In general, if the partners in a relationship are too short-term oriented, both parties will have an incentive to exploit each other as quickly as possible and exit the relationship. On the other hand, if the partners are too long-term oriented and don't periodically experience benefits, their motivation to stay in and support the relationship will wane . . . . The key is to develop a relationship in which the partners are able to respond to market or environmental changes yet have enough rigidity or structure to create stakes for both parties and motivate them to act in the best interest of their relationship.

Defining Supplier Roles

Much of the benefit of supply development lies in defining appropriate supplier roles, including improving integration of business processes through cooperative relationships. A supply strategy should therefore also define critical areas for supplier integration (Laseter, 1998). Efforts to improve supply integration may range from adding previous buyer or other supplier activities to the supplier relationship, shifting a subset of activities from one supplier to another that can perform them more efficiently or effectively, or even eliminating low-value activities that the customer demanded of the supplier. Among the earliest and most extensive efforts for supplier integration are those between Wal-Mart and Procter and Gamble, which have linked computer systems, shared marketing and sales information, and jointly modified existing or developed new products (Ellison, Zimmerman, and Forelle, 2005).

A supply strategy should also quantify prospective opportunities to justify resources for implementation and to keep plans consistent with rewards (Laseter, 1998). The expected timing of savings should also be identified for use in budgeting and setting long-term business plans. Both the Air Force and the Marine Corps are exploring ways to identify likely savings, their timing, and their budgetary effects (see, for example, Moore et al., 2004, and Moore et al., forthcoming).

The implementation plan for the supply strategy should define the activities, resources, and milestones for achieving its objectives. A Gantt chart outlining the timing of tasks (plotting the time it takes to accomplish each action) can facilitate implementation (Laseter, 1998). The first task is typically to discuss the new strategy with suppliers that may be more willing to cooperate once they understand the rationale for a set of actions.

Tailoring Tactics to Commodity Categories

In planning for likely supplier responses to supply strategies, buyers should differentiate according to the attractiveness of their account; the relative value of their business to suppliers (the variables suppliers use to develop their own strategies toward buyers); and, most importantly, the category of commodities involved. Below, we review potential buyer responses, as suggested by Steele and Court (1996), to supplier strategies for strategic, bottleneck, leverage, and noncritical commodities (see Figure 4.4) and as based on the relative value of the buyer's business and the attractiveness of the buyer's account for goods and services within each quadrant.[15]

Strategic. For strategic commodities (high value, high vulnerability), the buyer's objectives are to monitor supplier performance closely and to work to improve the relationship with the supplier. If the supplier sees the business as core to its own strategy, there is a good buyer-supplier match that the buyer will want to develop or encourage, particularly through partnerships or strategic alliances (Figure 5.4). If the supplier classifies the business as development, the buyer should work closely with the supplier to increase the extent and content of the business, such as seeking out other categories of business in which both parties are interested.

Buyers should be most concerned if a supplier views their business for strategic items as exploitable or a nuisance, because problems with supply or pricing for such

Figure 5.4
Buyer Responses to Supplier Segmentations of Strategic Items

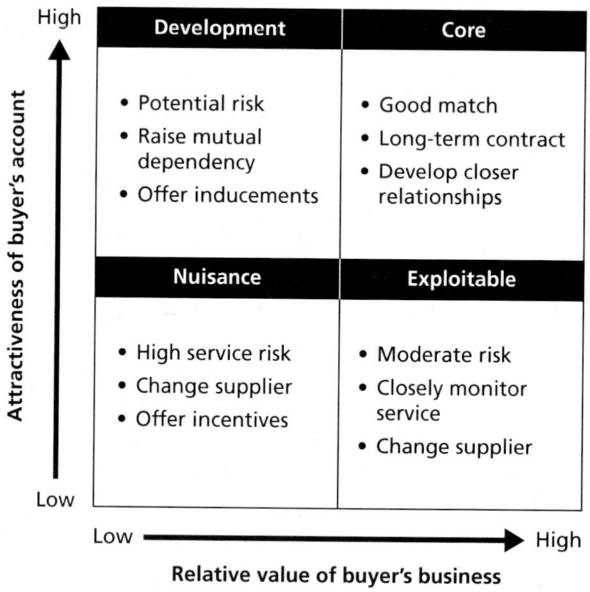

SOURCE: Adapted from Steele and Court (1996).
RAND *MG572-5.4*

---

15 For a case study of how a major chemical company implemented these tactics, see Gelderman and van Weele (2002).

goods cannot be changed easily. If feasible, the buyer should change suppliers that find its business for strategic items to be exploitable or a nuisance; if this is not feasible, the buyer will need to devote considerable time and attention to the relationship. If the supplier views the business as exploitable, the buyer should try to increase the level of mutual dependency, for instance, by sharing technology and innovations or creating jointly owned products, making it unattractive for the supplier to act as an adversary. If the supplier views the business as a nuisance, the buyer should try to make the business more attractive and provide the supplier with greater incentive to continue to do business. Examples of incentives include offering the prospect of ongoing profitable business; the certainty of prompt payment according to contractual terms; the prestige that can be derived through business with a leading organization; the use of simple procurement systems with straightforward, uncomplicated contracts; and opportunities to grow through the association.

Bottleneck. For bottleneck goods and services (low value, high vulnerability), the buyer seeks to ensure supply by establishing long-term contracts for which price is not a major consideration. If the supplier regards the buyer's business as core, the match is good, and both parties should be content to enter long-term contracts and develop closer relations (Figure 5.5). If the supplier regards the business as development, the buyer needs to increase mutual dependency so that the supplier increases commitment

Figure 5.5
Buyer Responses to Supplier Segmentations of Bottleneck Items

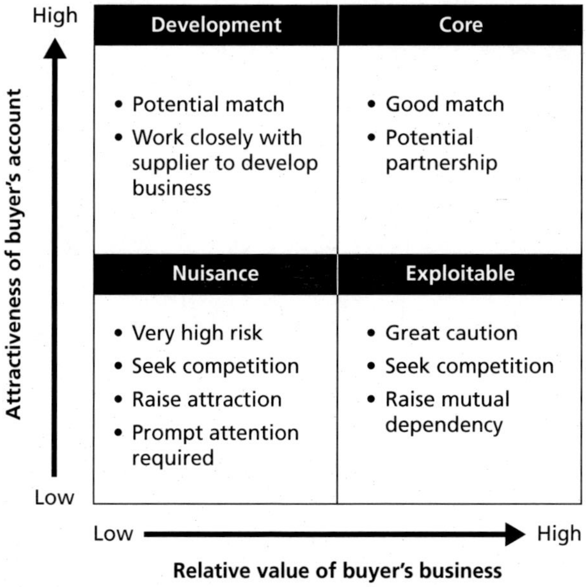

SOURCE: Adapted from Steele and Court (1996).
RAND *MG572-5.5*

to the relationship. A supplier that views the buyer for bottleneck commodities as a nuisance presents a very high-risk situation for buyers, including the possibility that the supplier will cease even limited production of the commodity. A buyer in such a situation should find a new supplier or, if this is not feasible, offer additional incentives, such as extra business or even higher prices in return for improved service. Should suppliers consider such business as exploitable; the buyer is at some risk of higher costs. Nevertheless, given that cost is not a principal consideration for bottleneck goods, buyers may want to maintain such relationships and perhaps increase mutual dependency, while preparing to change suppliers if high standards are not maintained.

Leverage. For leverage goods and services (high value, low vulnerability), buyers seek to increase profit. In all cases in which the supplier regards the business as core, there will be considerable commitment because the objectives of both buyer and seller are compatible even if not identical (Figure 5.6). The supplier will seek long-term contracts, while the buyer will prefer short-term contracts because of the abundant availability of goods and services from competitors. At the same time, the buyer needs to avoid antagonizing the supplier, perhaps by encouraging continued participation and interest or even currying supplier favor through long-term contracts for related commodities.

Figure 5.6
Buyer Responses to Supplier Segmentations of Leverage Items

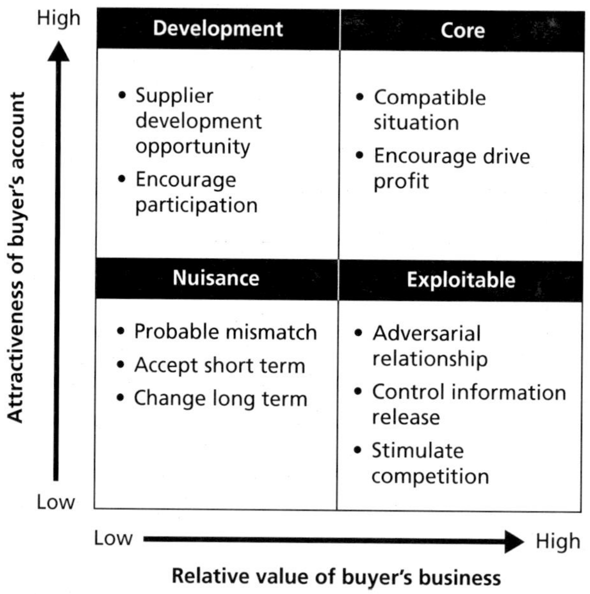

SOURCE: Steele and Court (1996). Copyright McGraw-Hill Companies, Inc. Used with permission.
RAND *MG572-5.6*

If a supplier considers the buyer's business for leverage goods and services as development, the buyer should develop and encourage the participation of other suppliers to increase and develop competition in the marketplace. Should suppliers of leverage goods and services view the buyer's business as a nuisance, the relationship is clearly a mismatch and will have a short term, with the buyer either changing suppliers or the supplier withdrawing from the market. If the supplier views a buyer's business for leverage commodities as exploitable, both parties are likely to focus on price, and the relationship is likely to be adversarial. Buyers should approach such suppliers with great care, tightly controlling the release of information and seeking competition wherever possible, given that such relationships are unlikely to be lasting or profitable.

Noncritical. For noncritical goods and services (low value, little supply risk), buyers seek to minimize attention to and develop greater efficiency in acquisitions through long-term contracts that give more responsibilities to the supplier. Buyers do better to focus on reducing administrative burdens rather than on price because even a large reduction in the purchase cost of these low-value goods will result in only a small savings in the total spend.

If a supplier regards a relationship with a buyer of noncritical goods and services as part of its core business, the match is very good, and the supplier can be expected to provide the attention that the buyer will not have to (Figure 5.7). Similarly, if a sup-

Figure 5.7
Buyer Responses to Supplier Segmentations of Noncritical Items

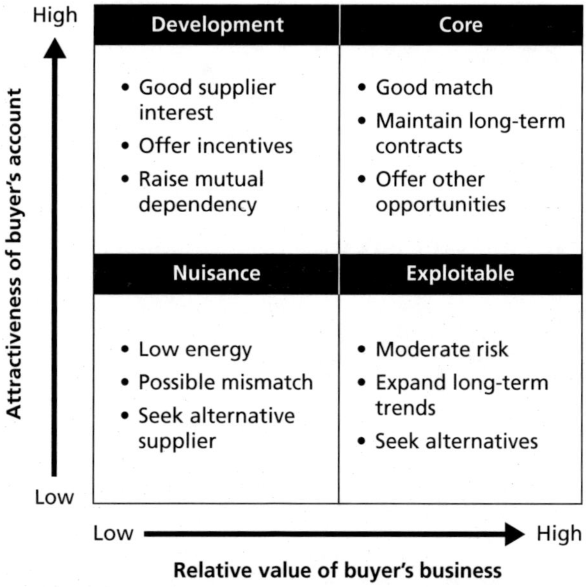

SOURCE: Adapted from Steele and Court (1996). Copyright McGraw-Hill Companies, Inc. Used with permission.
RAND *MG572-5.7*

plier regards a buyer's business for noncritical commodities as development, the match is likely good, and the buyer can improve it by offering incentives and raising mutual dependency. If a supplier regards a buyer's business for noncritical goods and services as a nuisance or exploitable, the buyer will likely have to resolve problems continually and overcome difficulties with trivial, nonstrategic purchases. Buyers may be able to improve supplier approaches to noncritical commodities by increasing payments in return for better service, although the buyer should continue to monitor the service and be prepared to change suppliers if necessary.

Evaluation and Planning

After considering options, reactions, and responses, the commodity council should also establish specific goals for evaluating the supply strategy's progress (Monczka, Trent, and Handfield, 2002). Such goals should directly relate to the objectives or requirements of the enterprise. In particular, the goals should be specific, measurable, and actionable; evaluate internal progress over time and compare performance to that of external competitors and benchmarks; extend beyond price to other variables affecting total cost; be established with the supplier, when appropriate; and evaluate quality, customer service, availability, and responsiveness. Goals should also be based on competitive analysis, comparison with marketplace leaders, and future marketplace trends. Other planning elements include establishing tasks to be completed and their timelines, assigning accountability and process ownership, ensuring adequate resources are available to process owners, developing a negotiation plan before meeting with suppliers, communicating the strategy to all users and stakeholders (and explaining the strategy to suppliers and internal customers), and developing a contingency plan if events do not occur as planned.

Document Strategy

Once the commodity council has finalized a strategy for a particular group of goods and services, it needs to document the strategy in writing and share it with all participants and other stakeholders in the process.

Step 13: Execute the Supply Strategy

Once the supply strategy has been developed and documented, it is executed. Execution involves identifying and prequalifying the best suppliers, issuing requests for proposals; selecting one or more suppliers; negotiating fact-based terms and conditions (based on analyses of high-quality data and reflecting actual costs, capacities, and processes of the supplier); finalizing the relationship, including performance metrics and incentives; managing the transition to new suppliers; and monitoring the performance of suppliers and the supply strategy. Many of these steps parallel those for letting a contract under traditional PSM processes. Our point in noting them here, in the last step of the process we outline, is to emphasize how much work must occur before an enterprise purchases a good or service. The specific process of letting the contract is but one part of the overall execution of a supply strategy, which must also include ongoing efforts to measure performance and monitor the supplier relationship.

In executing the supply strategy, the commodity council may view suppliers as attractive for a variety of financial, performance, technological, organizational, or strategic reasons (Olsen and Ellram, 1997, Table 4):

- financial and economic factors
  - margins
  - financial stability
  - scale and experience
  - barriers to entry and exit
  - slack
- performance factors
  - delivery
  - quality
  - price
- technological factors
  - ability to cope with changes in technology
  - types and depth of current and future technologies
  - current and future capacity utilization
  - design capabilities
  - speed in development
  - patent protection
- organizational, cultural, and strategic factors
  - influence on buyer's network position
  - internal and external integration of the supplier
  - strategic fit with buyer
  - management outlook for the future
  - top management capability
  - compatibility across buyer levels and functions
  - general risk and uncertainty for buyer
  - buyer feeling of trust
- other factors
  - ability to cope with environmental changes
  - safety record of supplier.

Many of these variables are the same variables that will influence buyers to choose one supplier over another. Enterprises should discuss each variable and weight their importance when assessing and selecting suppliers.

Similarly, the commodity council can assess several variables likely to determine the strength of the supply relationships they develop (Olsen and Ellram, 1997). Such variables include economic factors and the nature of the relationship, e.g., cooperation and distance between buyer and supplier (Olsen and Ellram, 1997):

- economic factors
  - volume or dollar volume of purchase
  - importance of buyer to supplier
  - exit costs
- character of exchange relationship
  - types of exchange
  - level and number of personal contacts
  - number of other partners
  - duration of exchange relationship
- cooperation between buyer and supplier
  - cooperation in development of new goods and services
  - technical cooperation
  - integration of management
- distance between buyer and supplier
  - social
  - cultural
  - technological
  - time, including speed of processes
  - geographic.

In selecting suppliers, the commodity council may weight the factors affecting supplier attractiveness and relationships and plot them against each other (Olsen and Ellram, 1997). Such weighting should be adapted to the market conditions for each commodity.[16]

If supplier attractiveness is stronger than the buyer-supplier relationship and if the supplier provides a strategically important commodity or if the purchase is difficult to manage, the commodity council may seek to improve the relationship through greater communication, providing suppliers with more volume, or involving them in product development (Olsen and Ellram, 1997). If the supplier relationship is relatively strong and the supplier moderately or highly attractive, commodity councils may wish to

[16] Use of standard weights for all commodities may "introduce an unwarranted element of scientific objectivity into a highly judgmental assessment process," one in which a variable (e.g., technological position) of minor importance in one market may be critical in another (Day, 1986, p. 200).

allocate resources to maintaining a strong relationship and look for ways to manage it more effectively.

If the supplier is not attractive, the commodity council may wish to consider different suppliers, although enterprises should consider the influence of the supplier on its network position, such as whether a new supplier's network will be equally effective. Other strategies may include outsourcing the purchase (for instance, outsourcing the purchase of some inputs, such as raw materials, component parts, or transportation to a distributor, contract manufacturer, or a third-party logistics provider) or using systems contracting to enhance supplier attractiveness. In many cases, particularly for bottleneck items, the commodity council may have an impetus to work with current or known suppliers and to improve relationships with them.

Once new suppliers are chosen, factors likely to affect the difficulty of managing the purchase include those related to the characteristics of the product, the supply market, and the supply environment (Olsen and Ellram, 1997):

- product characteristics
  - novelty
  - complexity
  - functional (number of parts and subassemblies)
  - manufacturing
  - specification
  - application
  - commercial
  - political
- supply market characteristics
  - suppliers' power
    - size
    - number of suppliers
    - resource dependence
    - lack of substitutions
  - suppliers' technical and commercial competence
- environmental characteristics
  - risk (opportunistic behavior, commercial, technological)
  - uncertainty (market, technical).

Changes in any of these may mean the purchase requires additional attention and monitoring.

The last component of execution is monitoring results and reviewing performances to verify that the strategy is achieving its stated objectives or to determine whether it requires modification (Monczka, Trent, and Handfield, 2002). Key elements of monitoring and review include conducting regular meetings to determine whether the strategy is well aligned with organizational objectives, sharing results with top management to ensure their continued support and to secure additional momentum for the strategy; assessing internal customer and supplier perceptions; determining whether key goals have been achieved; executing contingency plans if accomplishments are lacking; providing feedback and lessons learned to those involved; and assessing whether key assumptions underlying the strategy have changed significantly, making it necessary to revise the strategy.

Supply strategies are iterative. Firms constantly revisit and reassess their decisions in response to new information about demand and supply, supplier performance, customer needs, and other changes in market conditions.

CHAPTER SIX

Conclusions

Leading enterprises are making significant commitments to changing their PSM practices. They are analyzing their spending, segmenting it into major commodity groups based on some measure of value and vulnerability to the enterprise, and prioritizing them for initial PSM efforts. These enterprises use multifunctional teams to systematically develop sourcing strategies linked to the strategic goals of the enterprise. The exact steps may vary by enterprise, but most strategy development processes will contain many of the elements presented in this document.

The Air Force and DoD can use the means of developing, segmenting, and targeting goods, services, and suppliers and then developing supply strategies that we have outlined to develop tailored supply strategies that should better support the warfighter. In fact, both the Air Force and DoD have already launched initiatives based on many of the best practices we have discussed here.

The Air Force has developed a capability to do spend analyses and is beginning to develop supply strategies for a number of spending categories. These efforts are being implemented both across the Air Force and at the Air Force Materiel Command (AFMC). Both AFMC and Air Force–wide efforts use the same process for developing supply strategies. AFMC analyzed its spending and grouped the bulk of its purchases into eight major commodity groups. Air Force and AFMC methods for segmenting spend and prioritizing initiatives have varied.

Other services and agencies, including the Office of Federal Procurement Policy, the Defense Procurement and Acquisition Policy office, and the office of the Deputy Under Secretary of Defense for Logistics and Materiel Readiness, are also launching strategic sourcing initiatives to develop supply strategies for goods and services. In some cases, it may make sense to have multifunctional teams comprising members from across the federal government or DoD to develop federal or DoD-wide strategies. In others, it may make sense to have services or even major commands develop specific supply strategies. Regardless, supply segmentation and strategy development require a sound methodology for analyzing and segmenting spending, prioritizing and selecting initiatives, and developing and implementing strategies.

One of the primary benefits of segmenting spending is gaining detailed knowledge of one's own business. Beyond the goal of developing a future course of action, organizations benefit from simply completing the analysis—providing that their own personnel perform the analysis (Ellram, 2002). The complexity of the task suggests that a subcontractor cannot perform the task and achieve results as optimal as those that internal personnel with substantive expertise can provide. DoD needs to learn to do this by itself. Fortunately, it has the personnel to do so.

Ideally, supply segmentation and strategy development should be an interactive process that requires management participation to determine priorities, provide resources, help remove any barriers to implementation, resolve ambiguities, and determine which areas to pursue in depth and which to defer. This issue is particularly relevant for the Air Force, which has sometimes outsourced complex analyses. Air Force personnel learning and conducting supply strategies are most likely to provide the greatest long-term benefits to the service, particularly given the need to tailor analyses and strategies to differing commodity groups.

Although many activities are common to most supply strategies, no one process, segmentation framework, or supply strategy is likely to fit all enterprises and their commodities. A strategic approach that delivers the most rewards to the enterprise will require extensive and time-consuming data gathering and analysis, both across the entire enterprise and across the industries in which it does business.

One of the primary limitations of analyses for supply strategies is the inadequacy of using two-dimensional frameworks for researching complex interdependencies between two or more items. While two-dimensional frameworks like the one we have discussed here can help focus management attention on primary issues and suggest areas of potential improvements, they also require careful consideration of the interactions between the various dimensions of the PSM process and of possible unintended consequences of changing current methods of sourcing. Ignoring these interactions may result in failure to realize all expected savings and performance improvements or even unintended detrimental outcomes.

In closing, we note again this document synthesizes literature on developing supply strategies. While it provides a composite process and factors to consider when developing supply strategies, readers may wish to consult the references we cite for more context and further understanding of these topics. While there is no consensus on the right process, this document should help those designing supply strategies better understand what to do and help those who have been developing supply strategies further refine and improve their efforts.

APPENDIX A

A Process for Grouping Requirements in Developing Supply Strategies

Many requirements are interdependent or synergistic. That is, they require similar materials, technology, personnel or management skills or have lower total costs when purchased together rather than separately. For some commodities, savings are realized from economies of scale in production and administration. Consolidating interdependent activities into fewer contracts can also realize economies of scope (the total cost of certain goods and services, such as office supplies, integrated facilities management). Conversely, suppliers and contracts can become so large that diseconomies of scale or scope appear. Demands that exceed a supplier's capacity or capabilities or that require a supplier to expand too fast can lead to poor performance, just as demands that represent a high proportion of total supplier sales can lead to excessive dependency on the buyer and possible failure if buyer demands are suddenly reduced. Ideally, a buyer wants to find the points between economies and diseconomies of scale and scope (Baldwin, Camm, and Moore, 2001). In this appendix, we present a process for grouping requirements in developing supply strategies. Efforts to aggregate requirements for government goods and services are subject to regulations for "fair and open" competition, as well as other policy goals.[1]

Given the possible interdependencies and synergies among some goods and services, teams developing supply strategies need to consider not only the selected commodity group but prospective aggregations of other goods and services. For example, commodities may be grouped by common suppliers; their use in production, manufacturing, or maintenance; their personnel requirements; or their requirements in shipping and storage (such as temperature and shelf life). Commodities are especially suitable for grouping if there are high-quality suppliers that have the scale or scope to fulfill an

[1] A key consideration for "fair and open" competition, as required by the Competition in Contracting Act, is whether aggregated requirements are so large that only one company or supplier can bid. Nevertheless, Federal Acquisition Regulations allow suppliers to team to bid, as some have done for large weapon system contracts. Other federal regulations affecting aggregation of requirements, as noted in our discussion of identifying prospective opportunities for PSM initiatives across an enterprise, include limits on contract length and preferences for small businesses.

aggregation of requirements. Indeed, the DLA was created to aggregate requirements for common goods across DoD, just as the GSA does across the federal government.

Aggregating requirements can also reduce the supply base. A large supply base can naturally increase the variability of lead times, material consistency, interpretation of specifications and requirements, and transportation and delivery, adversely affecting supply-chain quality (Trent, 2001). Given the strategic necessity of managing supplier quality, a smaller supply base, if carefully selected, can help improve supply-chain performance (including such elements as quality, responsiveness, and reliability).

Care must be taken in aggregating requirements. Some parts of the sourcing process, for example, are more amenable to outsourcing than others. For example, while IBM, Hewlett-Packard (HP), and Motorola all outsource manufacturing to electronics manufacturing services or original design manufacturers, they control the sourcing of critical components more tightly to maintain direct relationships with the suppliers of these components, to maintain visibility into the supply chain, and to manage risk and gain procurement leverage (Carbone, 1999, 2001, and 2004).

Dimensions for Grouping Commodities

Requirements for goods and services can be grouped along one of four dimensions: by commodity group or subgroup, across commodity groups, across management levels, or over time. Grouping by any of these four, or a combination of them, can help improve performance and reduce transaction, administrative, and other related costs.

Aggregating by Commodity Group or Subgroup

The most obvious dimension for aggregating requirements is by commodity group or subgroup. For example, the requirements for bearings, wheels and brakes, or electronic warfare systems could be aggregated across suppliers or weapon systems, while the requirements for food service, pest control, or elevator repair could be aggregated across sites. Enterprisewide commodity requirements could be strategically consolidated, based on total ownership costs, with one or more high-performing suppliers. Many existing requirements for common goods and services could be consolidated across the Air Force or DoD. The Air Force or DoD could also develop one or more enterprisewide "umbrella" supplier relationships that would be available to any site manager, major command, or weapon system manager. Alternatively, an Air Force site manager, command, or weapon system manager could develop a prototype commodity relationship that could be expanded to other sites, commands, or weapon systems as trust grows in the supplier relationship. No single aggregation approach is likely to fit all goods and services.

Aggregating requirements by group or subgroup offers advantages in standardization of goods and services and information systems; economies of scale from leveraging core supplier competencies and reducing buyer and supplier transaction costs; and facilitation of benchmarking and process improvement across sites, suppliers, and end products, such as weapon systems. Nevertheless, such aggregation can also raise concerns about the availability and consistency of supplier performance (for example, quality, delivery, costs), need for diversity of requirements across end products (for example, particular need for weapon systems, such as systems integration) or sites (for example, need to meet regional preference for food or specific site requirements such as irrigation or snow removal).

Aggregating Across Commodity Groups

Groups of goods and services can also be aggregated by site, supplier, or end product (such as weapon systems). For example, weapon system sustainment requirements that are sole-sourced with an original equipment manufacturer (OEM) can be aggregated, as they have been for recent corporate contracts, such as those with General Electric, Boeing, and Lockheed Martin. Requirements for services, such as janitorial, groundskeeping, and plumbing services, can also be aggregated for a single site, as they have been at Vance Air Force Base, Oklahoma, and some other installations. Among the means for aggregating interrelated commodities are adding new commodities or responsibilities to existing contracts as trust in suppliers grows or aggregating commodities to match the portfolio of goods and services offered by companies that specialize in large-scale task management.[2] Alternatively, requirements can be aggregated into a very large group of commodities that could be purchased from an alliance of suppliers with complementary core competencies. Some complex weapon systems currently use such an acquisition process.

The advantages of consolidating requirements across interrelated commodity groups can include economies of scope (gained, for example, from cross-training personnel, such as training drivers to set up the equipment they deliver, or from sharing equipment), better alignment between buyer and supplier incentives,[3] improved coordination (such as having fewer contracts and suppliers to award, manage, and coordinate), improved accountability (such as having fewer overlaps of and gaps in respon-

---

[2] RAND researchers have observed three general types of suppliers: those that perform all activities included in the work scope, those that specialize in supplier management and subcontract the bulk of the work scope, and those that perform some of the work scope and subcontract the rest.

[3] For example, when DoD separated the insurance and service aspects of moving household goods, damage costs were twice those in the commercial marketplace. That is, combining the costs of insurance for moves with the costs of moving the goods helped reduce the former. When one Air Force installation separated carpet cleaning from janitorial services, one of its carpet-cleaning contractors shirked the required application of Scotch Guard that made carpets easier to maintain. Again, the costs of separating rather than aggregating the goods increased the total costs to the buyer, because the Air Force had to clean improperly treated carpets more often. Separating equipment maintenance costs from overhaul costs can also lead to suboptimal maintenance decisions (e.g., infrequent oil changes) that drive up overhaul costs.

sibility[4]), improved flexibility (the ability to adjust to actual requirements or changed priorities), and parallels with the original acquisition process that can aid the transition from acquisition to sustainment. Nevertheless, such aggregation can raise concerns about compromises on economies of scale (particularly if, for example, a technical expert might be required for every site or end product), the breadth of supplier core competencies,[5] and reductions in the number of businesses able to bid for a contract (for instance, many small businesses might not be able to bid directly on contracts for aggregated requirements).[6]

Aggregating Requirements Across Management Levels

Requirements can also be aggregated across management levels, either for major systems or sites. Recent examples include support for the F-117 and the C-17; engine rental contracts (for example, Rolls-Royce's "power-by-the-hour" agreements); the joint base operating support contract for the Kennedy Space Center and Patrick Air Force Base at Cape Canaveral, Florida; and the recent contract for management of test ranges.

There are two alternative ways to aggregate requirements across management levels. One is to slowly devolve management responsibility to existing suppliers as confidence and trust in them increase. Another is to strategically consolidate management requirements for award to one lead supplier. Within DoD, for example, this can involve delegating responsibility to a prime contractor to manage subcontractors, as has occurred in many performance-based logistics contracts, rather than directly managing contracts with many different individual suppliers.

Figure A.1 illustrates these approaches for facilities services. Firm 1 manages some internal providers and a number of specialized vendors that provide different services. Firm 2 has a provider that provides some services but largely manages independent vendors for the buyer. Firm 3 has a provider that provides many different services and manages several subcontractors for it. Firm 4 has an alliance of several large providers that provide most services but that also manage a specialty vendor for it and several of their own subcontractors.

---

4 For example, one reason Microsoft aggregated its diverse facility management contracts was because it found that, for some services, either no one provider was responsible or multiple providers were (Ouellette and Pettinger, 1997).

5 For example, weapon system support, logistics, and facility management services each encompass such a broad range of services, and no one firm in these industries is likely to perform all these services, much less perform them all well. That is, suppliers may have core competencies in a subset of goods and services within these industries but rarely in all the services within each industry. The British Ministry of Defence has moved away from very broad contracts for installation support services and toward contracts better matching the capabilities of leading suppliers. It has also begun encouraging or requiring offers by consortia of firms.

6 Nevertheless, businesses can form teams to bid on a contract with a broad scope of work, and small businesses can be subcontractors to larger suppliers. Defense contractors often form teams to bid on major weapon system acquisitions. Major facility management companies have also formed teams to bid on a contract with a broad scope of work, as have major logistics companies. See Bradley (1997) for a specific logistics example.

Figure A.1
An Illustration of Alternative Ways to Aggregate Facilities Services Requirements Across Management Levels

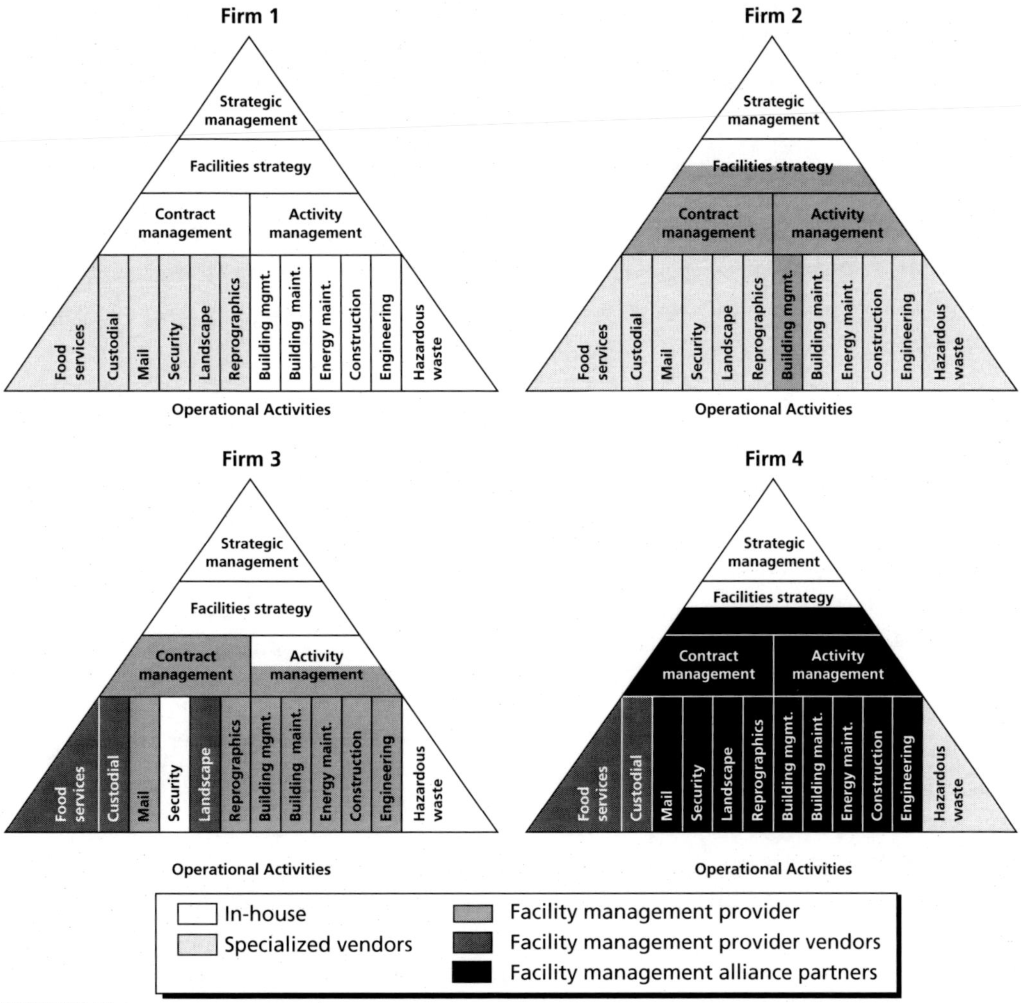

RAND *MG572-A.1*

Advantages of aggregating requirements across management levels include improving alignment of incentives for buyer and supplier, leveraging of supplier investments in integrated management systems, encouraging creativity and innovative new ideas (for example, making decisionmaking more flexible and lines of accountability and responsibility clearer), and avoiding some government constraints (such as those for selecting and managing subcontractors). Such aggregation can raise concerns regarding devolving management to suppliers, including reducing the sense of control, threatening jobs of many functional managers (including those often involved in developing major sourcing strategies) for the buyer, and reducing training opportunities. To assuage concern over a perceived loss of managerial control, many leading suppliers have developed extensive systems for monitoring and measuring their performance. Reduced training opportunities can be of particular concern to the Air Force because they also reduce the opportunities for training the managers of these goods and services. Among the possible means of mitigating this concern are training with industry programs for junior and midlevel personnel and hiring experienced outside personnel for civilian positions.

Aggregating Requirements Across Time

Finally, requirements can be aggregated over time through multiyear contracts, which reduce total costs and encourage both the buyer and the supplier to invest in the relationship (Artman and Martha, 1998). Longer-term relationships may help align purchasing activities with the overall strategic goals of an enterprise, particularly for goods and services with highly variable demand (and resulting uncertainty over the supply relationship). Increasing investments and commitment to a longer-term relationship can help reduce costs and improve performance over the life of a contract, including reductions in variance, defects, and lead times (Hahn, Kim, and Kim, 1986).

Figure A.2 is a notional illustration of the effects of combining contracts on total costs. In this example, five identical one-year contracts are combined with one supplier and then are extended to five years with the application of additional best purchasing practices. The bar to the far left shows these five identical contracts stacked, with three cost components for each: buyer transaction costs, provider transaction costs, and actual production costs. The column immediately to the right of this column, identical in height, groups the three categories of costs. The middle column illustrates the effects of contract and supplier consolidation, that is, of leverage and economies of transactions, scale, and scope realized by combining the five one-year contracts into one one-year contract. Transaction costs go down for both the buyer and supplier as the buyer gains additional leverage and the supplier gains some economies of scale in production. The bar to the right of the middle bar illustrates the effects of cost spreading and the learning-curve benefits of extending a one-year contract to five years. One-time buying and selling transaction costs are lower because they are now spread over five years rather than incurred every year; the supplier learns to reduce production costs as well. The far right column illustrates the benefits of both periodic and continuous supply-chain improvement resulting from the application, in the extended contract, of best PSM practices, such as performance incentives, supplier development, and supplier integration.

Similarly, Figure A.3 is a notional illustration of the benefits that can result from reducing supplier variance, lead time, and defects when combining contracts with suppliers providing similar products. Overall performance is likely to improve as contracts are combined with the best supplier. The buyer gains further leverage with this supplier, resulting in additional benefits. When the contract is extended from one to five

Figure A.2
Notional Example of How Aggregating Requirements Can Reduce Total Costs

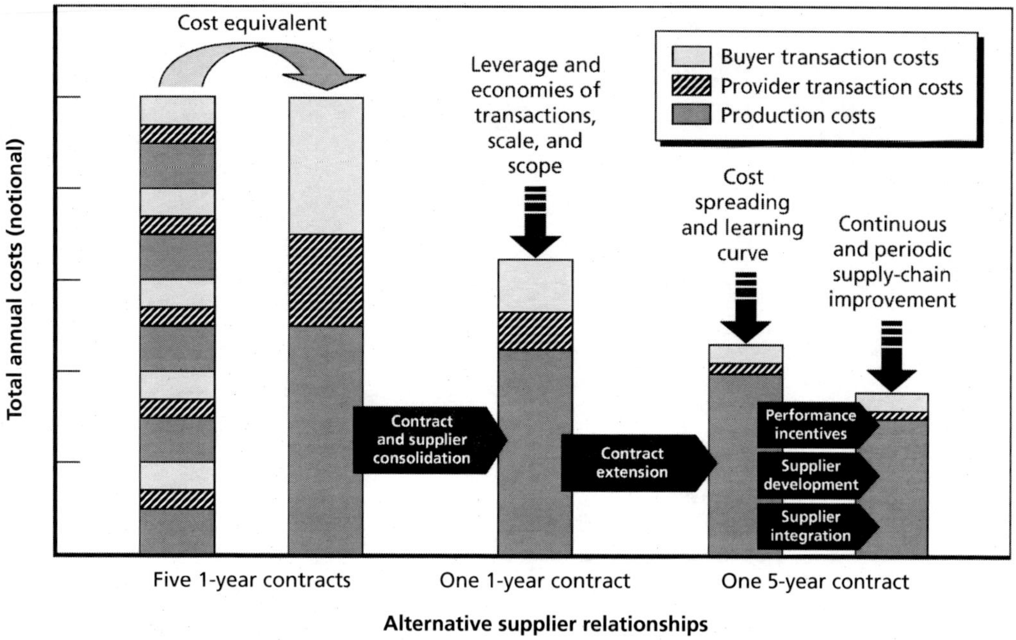

NOTE: Transaction costs have been exaggerated for illustration. While consolidation and changing contract terms do not always produce savings of the magnitudes or in the categories illustrated above, these options should be considered because they can further reduce costs and improve performance.
RAND *MG572-A.2*

years, supplier performance further improves as the supplier proceeds along a learning curve. Finally, when performance incentives, supplier development, and supplier integration are applied, the buyer experiences continuous and periodic improvements in supplier performance.

In addition to promoting continuous improvement, other advantages of aggregating requirements over time include justifying additional resources for customizing supplier relationships and enabling suppliers to recover investments in specific assets or services and improvement initiatives. For large, complex contracts, it can take a new service supplier a year or more to learn the buyer's operations (for example, its processes, cost, and performance information) well enough to identify where performance can be improved and costs reduced.

Concerns of requirements aggregation over time include loss of competitive incentives, dated industry intelligence, and limited opportunities for new suppliers. Nevertheless, periodic benchmarking of supplier costs and performance can help maintain competitive incentives and update industry intelligence. In many industries, consulting firms or academic organizations can also help update industry intelligence as needed for buyers.

Figure A.3
Notional Example of How Aggregating Requirements Can Improve Performance

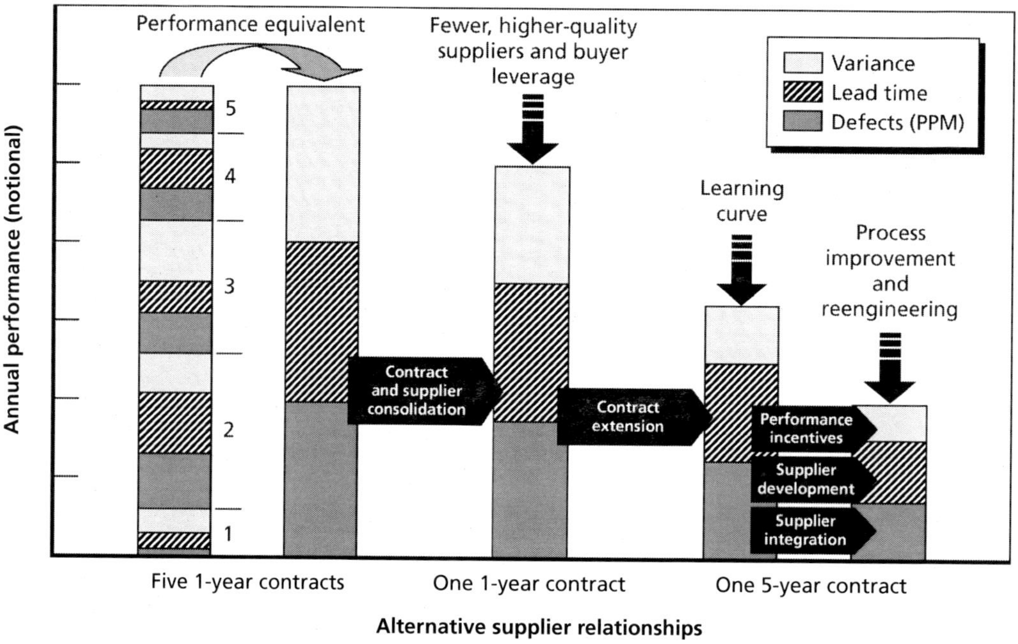

NOTE: While consolidation and changing contract terms do not always produce savings of the magnitudes or in the categories illustrated above, these options should be considered because they can further reduce costs and improve performance.
RAND *MG572-A.3*

A Process for Aggregating Requirements

Requirements for purchasing can be handled reactively, as they arise, just as traditional purchasing organizations handle customer demands. Meeting requirements in this way, however, can lengthen customer lead times and miss significant opportunities for improving performance and reducing costs. Furthermore, it can be difficult to align the purchasing activities of an enterprise with its overall strategic goals when PSM personnel are dealing with daily "fires."

Successful supply managers know that waiting for a request to come limits the number of creative solutions that can be implemented (Roberts, 2002). Indeed, purchasing needs to become more proactive in ensuring supply when demand is highly uncertain, as it is for many weapon system components, for which forecasting often falls short of effectively and efficiently meeting customer needs.[7]

[7] Crawford (1988) found that Air Force demands for aircraft spare parts are highly variable and change over time, with the number of parts in the repair pipeline over time being even more variable than the number of

One way to do this is to seek out, when possible, suppliers that are more flexible and responsive and to establish relationships with them, as well as to develop processes that link suppliers to the ultimate customer. Given the many dimensions for aggregating or grouping requirements, some of which may be mutually exclusive (for instance, *across* or *within* sites or weapon systems), a process is needed to help structure and make aggregation decisions.

Buyer Considerations

In considering how to structure and make requirements aggregation decisions, buyers need to consider four variables. Buyers need to understand

1. the *needs of internal and external customers*, including those for customization or flexibility of goods and services and their willingness to delegate or consolidate authority
2. the *strategic goals of the enterprise*, including, in the case of the Air Force and DoD, goals for small business and disadvantaged business utilization, and how they will be affected by aggregating requirements
3. the *capabilities and capacities of prospective suppliers*, including their core competencies by activity, location, and for final products[8]
4. the *options available in supplier relationships*, including how much capacity or capability suppliers can quickly add and the management responsibilities suppliers could assume without adversely affecting performance or the attractiveness of the buyer to suppliers.

Elements of Plan for Aggregation

Beyond the considerations buyers must make in evaluating requirements aggregation, a plan for aggregation should include the following four elements:

- a plan for learning
- reengineering
- balancing customer needs, supplier capabilities, and risks
- balancing supplier relationship options.

---

demands. The author concluded that excessive demand variability substantially reduces the confidence that can be placed in requirements and capability assessment models; in particular, mean variation in repair pipelines higher than that assumed by requirements models has a damaging effect on aircraft availability and wartime readiness.

[8] Some suppliers, for example, may be good at making or repairing some items but not those with more advanced technology. Others may be excellent providers of services in one region but have little or no experience elsewhere. Buyers should also understand how suppliers achieve economies of scale or scope.

Plan for Learning. Requirements aggregation is dynamic and interactive; consequently, buyers need a plan for learning. By starting with the easiest and least risky aggregations and moving to more-challenging ones over time, buyers can build on their successes and learn from their mistakes. Buyers should allow for growth and shrinkage of a specific grouping of requirements over time. They will want to increase the devolution of responsibility as their trust increases in suppliers and their sourcing strategies. Over time, buyers may want to develop prototypes for several different types of requirements groupings, as the Air Force has done with its support relationships for the C-17 and F-117.

Reengineering. Requirements may be grouped in ways that are structurally inefficient or ineffective. This may impede performance improvements, measurement, and management, and misalign incentives. To reduce the risks of this and to increase the rewards of aggregation, buying enterprises may want to reengineer current processes to improve performance measurement, create clear boundaries and interfaces, reduce "touch points" throughout the value chain, and match best industry practices and requirements aggregations.

For example, to simplify and shorten its parts delivery process, Sun Microsystems aggregated its service parts storage with repair activities and repair requirements (White, 2002). As a result, it reduced its repair suppliers from 80 to 12 and eliminated two warehouses. Now, Sun repair technicians ship broken service parts directly to repair vendors. Vendors then ship serviceable parts directly to remote stock locations. Sun reports that, between FYs 2000 and 2002, this helped the company save more than $21 million, reduced its number of transactions by five million, reduced its inventory from more than $280 million to less than $220 million, and improved local levels of parts availability from 92 to 98 percent.

Nike offers another example of requirements aggregation and reengineering that helped improve processes (Motley, 1995). In 1992, Nike had 25 distribution centers dispersed throughout Europe. Because Nike products have a short shelf life, the company was plagued in some regions by a shortage of popular models, resulting in lost sales, and overstock of other models, leading to steep discounting to dispose of product. An analysis of markets and geography concluded that one large, centralized distribution center would better serve Nike's customers, smooth its uneven regional demands, and reduce its total logistics costs.

Reengineering can also help buyers improve internal processes before developing new sourcing strategies and obtain better information for sourcing decisions. Buyers may not always understand or measure well their internal activities or processes. Some activities may no longer be needed, while others could be restructured. By reorganizing internal activities to better match current market practices and structures, buyers are better able to compare internal costs and performance and interfaces with suppliers. If outsourcing is an option, some buyers choose to reorganize and improve processes to shrink the pool of personnel that might be affected by it. This can help reduce problems with unions and local communities should outsourcing eventually occur.

Some buyers may choose to forgo process reengineering before developing sourcing strategies, particularly if the capital, labor, or time required for internal improvements is high or if outsourcing is a likely option. Many firms find it easier and quicker to obtain continuous performance improvements by shifting from internal to external suppliers. Buyers that undertake process reengineering simultaneously with initiation of a new supply strategy need to carefully structure the aggregation of requirements in a way that aligns incentives with reengineering goals and that a new organization structure does not eliminate opportunities for improvement (such as investments, consolidations, and training). The larger the aggregation of requirements and the longer the planned supplier relationship, the less likely it is that buyers will need to explore process reengineering before sourcing, assuming suppliers have been given proper incentives to continually reduce costs and to improve performance by reengineering their own processes.

Balancing Customer Needs, Supplier Capabilities and Preferences, and Risk. Buyers can follow a six-step process for balancing customer needs, supplier capabilities and preferences, and risks for more than one site or for an end product, such as a weapon system:

1. Identify candidate requirements for aggregation or disaggregation and supply strategy development.
2. Identify requirements reflecting the customer's most important priorities, needs, and risks.
3. Assess customer requirements and preferences for lower-priority requirements.
4. Analyze supplier capabilities and preferences for the most important customer requirements (as identified in step 2) and for any requirements that are typically coproduced.
5. Form requirement clusters by balancing the importance of the customer's priorities, needs, and risks (as identified in step 3) with supplier capabilities and preferences (as identified in step 4).
6. Identify any specialist suppliers worth keeping.

The following paragraphs describe each of these in turn.

Identify Candidate Requirements for Aggregation or Disaggregation and Supply Strategy Development. These requirements can be drawn from a spend analysis of existing contracts for related requirements and any prospective candidates for sourcing competition. Requirements can be aggregated by site or weapon system, across sites or weapon systems, or both. Leading practices in the private sector for aggregation of similar requirements can be used for initial aggregation, as can commodities that are already aggregated in existing supplier relationships. Prospective sourcing risks for each requirement within the initial aggregation should be determined, then requirements should be grouped into sourcing risk categories from lowest to highest. Within each sourcing risk group, requirements should be ranked according to prospective payoff (such as performance improvements, cost reductions) from more-innovative sourcing. Those requirements with the lowest risks and highest prospective payoffs should be the initial candidates for requirements aggregation.

Identify Requirements Reflecting the Customer's Most Important Priorities, Needs, and Risks. These should be drawn from the list of candidate requirements for aggregation. These are the requirements most important to the customer's mission or that require very high or special performance (such as high reliability, responsiveness, quality, and flexibility). For aggregating requirements across sites, this would be the most important location or the location at which performance is most important. For aggregating requirements within a site, this would be the most important purchased goods and services at the site. For aggregation across weapon systems, this might be the weapon system that must have the highest mission capability. For aggregation within a weapon system, this might be the most important subsystem. Aggregation across sites or weapon systems can be built around these high performance requirements, and additional requirements can be added to the aggregation as costs dictate. These requirements will be at the core of the prospective requirements aggregation.

Assess Customer Requirements and Preferences for Lower-Priority Requirements. Such requirements may not need high performance or customization. For aggregation across sites or weapon systems, customers are likely to be most concerned about standardization, specific suppliers, common contractual terms, responsiveness, and flexibility for such requirements, particularly for unique site or end-product needs. For aggregating requirements within sites or end products, such as weapon systems, customers are also likely to want a single point of contact to work issues of coordination and accountability.

Analyze Supplier Capabilities and Preferences for the Most Important Customer Requirements (as identified in Step 2) and for Any Requirements That Are Typically Coproduced. This includes market research to identify the pool of prospective suppliers and any unique or highly specialized suppliers and their capabilities (those for surge or customization, for instance, as well as their breadth of goods and services) and performance. It also includes an assessment of supplier preferences (such as strategy) to provide specific goods and services to the buyer. The goal of this step is to achieve the best match between core supplier competencies and preferences and the customer's highest priorities, needs, and risks, as well as to identify additional requirements (such as economies of scope, scale, or use of shared assets) that top supplier candidates might also support.

Form Requirement Clusters by Balancing the Importance of the Customer's Priorities, Needs, and Risks (as identified in Step 3) with Supplier Capabilities and Preferences (as identified in Step 4). This will identify the minimum number of aggregations of requirements to ensure high performance of critical activities, risk management, user preferences for standardization or customization, accountability, ease of interaction and management, and economies of scale and scope.

Identify Any Specialist Suppliers Worth Keeping. This step is to ensure that, in developing the right aggregation of requirements, a buyer does not overlook current suppliers (particularly local ones) that have consistently delivered high performance and gained the trust of customers. These suppliers would be evaluated to determine whether they are worth keeping because of specific site needs, customer preferences or other goals (e.g., small business preferences), or their ability to expand service areas. If retaining these specialist suppliers, buyers may want to increase the minimum number of aggregations of requirements or to see whether their capabilities can be expanded to accommodate an aggregation of requirements. Care must be taken in asking a specialty supplier to expand its capabilities to accommodate a broader aggregation of requirements. The Air Force and DoD, for example, can overwhelm the capabilities of small suppliers if they expand the scopes of their contracts too much or too fast. Buyers may also consider the possibility of specialist suppliers becoming subcontractors to a larger supplier.

Balancing Sourcing Options

Buyers must identify all relevant laws, regulations, and policies that may prevent the desired aggregation of requirements. For example, the Small Business Reauthorization Act of 1997 requires that any federal (including Air Force or DoD) aggregation of existing contracts be justified and produce measurably substantial benefits (Baldwin, Camm, and Moore, 2001). The requirements aggregation can be incrementally adjusted, if necessary, until it complies with all regulations. This will yield the most feasible and innovative requirements aggregation. Supply strategies for each aggregation of requirements can then be developed using the methodologies described in the main text.

APPENDIX B

Organizing for Supply Strategy Development

The goals of the PSM organization should directly support those of the enterprise. To do this, PSM organizations develop supply strategies to support an enterprise's strategic goals while conforming to the commercial, cultural, and regulatory environments within which it operates. In this appendix, we discuss alternative organizational structures for PSM organizations to facilitate supply strategy development, with attention to how organizational structure can affect support of enterprise goals.

We begin first with an overview of the advantages and disadvantages of centralized and decentralized structures, as well as of alternative structures that seek to combine these approaches. Second, we summarize several surveys of recent industry practices in PSM organization, including one of aerospace and defense industries. Third, we present seven examples of the organization of PSM activities at large companies. Fourth, we present a framework for deciding where to locate enterprisewide supply strategy teams (the location could, for example, be enterprise's headquarters or an SBU).[1]

Decentralization, Centralization, and Hybrid Approaches

The organization of purchasing depends greatly on the characteristics of the company and of the commodities it buys (van Weele, 1995). Most standard supply textbooks describe the advantages and disadvantages of centralized and decentralized supply organizational structures. Dobler and Burt (1996) notes that decentralization offers advantages in speed of operation, effective use of local sources, and plant autonomy, while centralization offers advantages of greater buyer specialization, consolidation of requirements, easier purchasing coordination and control, and effective planning and research.

[1] Much of the work presented here leverages previous unpublished research for the Army on consolidation of indirect spend.

Decentralization

Leenders et al. (2002) presents among the most complete analyses of the advantages and disadvantages of decentralization and centralization in purchasing (Tables B.1 and B.2). If purchasing goals include speed of operation, effective use of local sources, precisely satisfying the needs of local end users or internal customers, and visibility of operations, decentralization, because of its advantages, is logical for developing supply strategies. Decentralization can also help make more-effective use of local resources while spreading the total cost of supply management across units. In a widespread enterprise, or one comprising independent business units, local procurement and management may be the best way to satisfy local needs (Steele and Court, 1996). Decentralization can also enable close coordination and integration of design and operations with some key suppliers.

Table B.1
Potential Advantages and Disadvantages of Decentralization

Potential Advantages	Potential Disadvantages
Easier coordination and communication with operating department	More difficult to communicate among business units
Speed of response	Encourages users not to plan ahead
	Operational versus strategic focus
Effective use of local sources	Too much focus on local sources—ignores better supply opportunities
	No critical mass in organization for visibility and effectiveness—"whole-person syndrome"
	Lacks clout
Business unit autonomy	Suboptimization
	Business unit preferences not congruent with corporate preferences
	Small differences get magnified
Reporting line simplicity	Reporting at low level in organization
Undivided authority and responsibility	Limits functional advancement opportunities
Suits purchasing personnel preference	Ignores larger organization considerations
Broad job definition	Limited expertise for requirements
Geographical, cultural, political, environmental, social, language, currency appropriateness	Lack of standardization
Hide the cost of supply	Costs of supply relatively high

SOURCE: Leenders et al. (2002). Copyright McGraw-Hill Companies, Inc. Used with Permission.

Table B.2
Potential Advantages and Disadvantages of Centralization

Potential Advantages	Potential Disadvantages
Greater buying specialization	Narrow specialization and job boredom
	Lack of job flexibility
Ability to pay for talent	Corporate staff appears excessive
Consolidation of requirements—clout	Tendency to minimize legitimate differences in requirements
Coordination and control of policies and procedures	Lack of recognition of unique needs
Effective planning and research	Focus on corporate requirements, not on business unit strategic requirements
	Most knowledge sharing one way
Common suppliers	Even common suppliers behave differently in geographic and market segments
Proximity to major organizational decisionmakers	Distance from users
Critical mass	Tendency to create organizational silos
Firm brand recognition and stature	Customer segment require adaptability to unique situations
Reporting line—power	Top management not able to spend time on suppliers
Strategic focus	Lack of business unit focus
Cost of purchasing low	High visibility of purchasing costs

SOURCE: Leenders et al. (2002). Copyright McGraw-Hill Companies, Inc. Used with Permission.

Centralization

While decentralization can help develop local approaches and solutions to local sourcing problems, centralization can help reduce costs. A former IBM CEO cites centralized purchasing as one of the first things a company should do to save money (Gerstner, 2002). Consolidating common purchases has recently produced a wave of procurement savings (Stephens, 2005). More generally, given its advantages, centralization may be suitable if the purchasing goals are to maximize an enterprise's buying power (such as its leverage), reduce its total costs and risks, present a unified front to suppliers, or integrate buyer and supply systems. Centralization can also help foster standardization and joint continuous improvement throughout the value chain; minimize the resources required to perform rigorous spend analyses and technical commodity research; manage suppliers; and aid economic, industry, supplier, and risk analyses. Centralization can be particularly important when there are many small purchases because the benefits from consolidating requirements that are met through many small purchases are more significant than the benefits of consolidating large requirements. At the same time, centralization also has possible disadvantages—such as purchasing personnel becoming too narrowly specialized, the distance between users and suppliers increasing, and having executives seeking to economize any way possible not understand how the costs are aggregated.

Unsophisticated executives often mandate coordination across all business units to ensure maximum negotiating leverage, but such mandates are misguided because leverage is only one of a number of sourcing opportunity levers (Laseter, 1998). For example, opportunities for improving supply-chain management through such efforts as coordinated planning, forecasting, and replenishment or improving the leveraging of suppliers' innovation by involving them in product design, may require strong involvement at the business-unit level to be effective. Process efficiency argues for centralization, but aggregating demands enterprisewide complicates the effort and slows down the process. There is no single best answer because the balance between centralized and decentralized control varies by commodity.

Hybrid Approaches

A hybrid organizational structure, one with varying degrees of centralized authority and responsibility for purchasing and related functions but decentralized execution, can capture the benefits of both centralized and decentralized approaches. Such an approach may allow "evolution" through "devolution," in which "much of the more straightforward buying activity" is decentralized, while the corporate purchasing function "retain[s] and develop[s] its strategic contribution" (Baily et al., 2005, p. 5).

In center-led procurement, different purchasing models, including centralized shared-service, decentralized, and hybrid buying models, may be applied depending on what is bought, who needs it, and where it will be used (Stephens, 2005). This provides the benefit of decoupling purchasing management and execution processes, enabling them to be done in the most effective way. Common manufacturing components may be centrally sourced by purchasing, while needs for local facility services, such as snow removal, are addressed in local markets. In such an approach, even a commodity managed decentrally can still benefit from a central purchasing organization that focuses on high-value activities, such as the enterprise's continuous adoption of evolving best practices and innovations, developing contract templates, and researching commodity categories.

Some enterprises centralize the development of sourcing policy and processes and personnel development and training for PSM but do not centralize supply strategy development, purchasing, or supply management. Steele and Court (1996) notes that, given trends toward establishing autonomous business units within large conglomerates, the chief purchasing officer may be accountable for "functional excellence," with full, unlimited authority to monitor, evaluate, and change operations, standards, and personnel but not necessarily to undertake commitments with specific suppliers.

Other enterprises may also centralize some or all supply strategy development for the goods and services for which it makes sense to have large global, national, or regional contracts. Enterprisewide commodity councils for these goods and services could be located either in a central headquarters organization or, alternatively (especially when suppliers are closely involved in product design), at a key business unit or location. These teams perform rigorous analyses of requirements (including specifications and projected demands), spend, market, industry, and suppliers for selected commodities and develop proactive supply strategies to leverage total spending, lower total costs, manage risks, and improve performance. Given these strategies, the team then selects, negotiates, and establishes supply relationships (perhaps by writing contracts). Finally, central headquarters or the enterprisewide commodity team measures and manages supplier performance.

In this approach, actual purchasing is delegated to designated personnel in business or local operating units, to which the hybrid organizational structure gives command and control. This is somewhat similar to the use of GSA schedule contracts, which are specifically designed to enable purchasing by other federal organizations, although these GSA supplier relationships are not typically structured to fully leverage the purchasing power of the federal government.

Even when delegating actual purchasing authority, the central PSM organizations of many hybrid enterprises strongly encourage the business and operating units to use central supplier agreements that have been negotiated to reduce total costs and improve performance for the enterprise. Off-contract purchases are allowed if local purchasing personnel can demonstrate that the centralized agreement does not meet critical local operating needs. The hybrid structure thereby allows operating unit managers to make critical purchases that centralized agreements do not provide. This could have particular appeal to DoD; as the Defense Procurement Concept of Operations notes, "Ultimately, DoD's three services and other independent agencies must determine appropriate strategies based on their specific levels and requirements. Thus, primary control of commodity sourcing strategies should remain at the service level" (DoD, 2005, p. 18). The benefits of a hybrid approach for large enterprises with multiple business units or divisions is in achieving the advantages of standardization and volume leverage, where appropriate, yet also enabling close supplier relationships for design, planning, forecasting, and replenishment. A hybrid approach also assigns direct accountability to the specific business units or locations with the greatest stake in supply-chain performance and in ensuring suppliers support enterprise objectives.

Successfully executing a hybrid approach requires educating managers of business units, operating units, and facilities and their functional and contracting personnel on the benefits of centralized supplier agreements and the effects on total costs (not just price) of local purchasing decisions. It also requires a good data system to track purchases on and off contract to encourage compliance, including discerning the causes of off-contract "maverick" buying.

Industry Trends

Decentralized, centralized, and hybrid PSM organizations are all prevalent in the private sector. We next review recent reports of trends in purchasing organizations.

Changes in corporate approaches to purchasing, such as total corporate spend control, first started emerging on a large scale in the mid-1990s (Porter, 2003). The adoption of new purchasing approaches coincided with the emergence of the structural economic and business changes wrought by globalization and the outsourcing of non-core activities. While many companies kept their buying power decentralized, most seem to be moving toward total spend control, seeking a hybrid system that combines "the free-wheeling style of a decentralized purchasing operation with the 'critical intelligence' and buying muscle provided by centralization" (Porter, 2003). Authoritative, center-led PSM organizations, sometimes with direct-line reporting to the CEO, were found in 2002 to be one of six common practices leading firms were pursuing that were resulting in savings from 3 to 7 percent per year on spending for corporate goods and services (Porter, 2002).

A 2003 survey of 284 U.S. and Canadian companies found five structural categories for purchasing organizations (Johnson and Leenders, 2004):

- *centralized*—all or almost all purchase dollars are committed at one central location for the entire firm
- *centralized hybrid*—more than 50 percent of purchase dollars are committed at one central location for the entire firm
- *hybrid*—approximately 50 percent of purchase dollars are committed at one central location for the entire firm
- *decentralized hybrid*—less than 50 percent of purchase dollars are committed at one central location for the entire firm
- *decentralized*—all or almost all purchase dollars are committed on a divisional or plant basis for the entire company.[2]

Forty-one percent of respondents reported using a centralized hybrid structure, while 67 percent reported using one of the three hybrid structures. The use of hybrid structures has increased over time, as organizations have tried to harness the advantages of both centralized and decentralized structures with varying degrees of centralized authority and responsibility for purchasing and its related functions, coupled with decentralized execution (Table B.3). The survey also found that service-sector firms

---

[2] Definitions are verbatim from the questionnaire that Johnson and Leenders distributed to firms.

Table B.3
Supply Organizational Structure (percent)

Organizational Structure	1987	1995	2003
Centralized	28	23	26
Hybrid[a]	59	65	67
Decentralized	13	12	8

SOURCE: Johnson and Leenders, 2004.

[a] Centralized hybrid and decentralized hybrid were not options in 1987 and 1995 surveys. For comparability, these two categories have been combined with hybrid in the 2003 survey.

(31 percent) reported using centralized structures more often than manufacturing firms (22 percent) and that those with sales greater than $10 billion (53 percent) were less likely to use centralized or centralized hybrid purchasing organizations than those with sales up to $10 billion (70 percent). The survey investigators suggest such findings may provide evidence that organizations of a certain size or global reach may find it difficult or ineffective to centralize supply organizations.

A CAPS Research (2004) analysis of procurement organizations for 37 large corporations such as 3M, Caterpillar, HP, IBM, and Procter & Gamble found that

- 12 had centralized organizations in which the authority and responsibility for most purchasing and purchasing-related functions are assigned to a central organization
- 6 had decentralized organizations in which the authority and responsibility for most purchasing and purchasing-related functions are dispersed throughout the organization
- 19 had hybrid organizations with centralized sourcing and decentralized execution
- none outsourced or had most purchasing and purchasing-related activities performed by an external organization.

A more-focused CAPS Research (2005) analysis of procurement among 17 aerospace and defense industry firms found a preference for centralized purchasing organizations, especially for indirect goods, though this may be a result of how the data were reported, with individual SBUs, some within the same parent company, reporting "corporate"-level data.[3] The findings of the survey of aerospace and defense "firms" found that

[3] In the CAPS Research survey of 37 large corporations, 28 reported at the corporate level; in the survey of 17 aerospace and defense firms, only two did so. Among the defense and aerospace "firms" participating in the

- 7 respondents used centralized organizations to purchase direct goods and 11 for indirect goods
- 4 respondents used decentralized organizations for direct goods and 3 for indirect goods
- 5 respondents used hybrid organizations for direct goods and 3 for indirect goods
- no respondents used outsourcing for direct or indirect goods.[4]

Again, we caution that the differing context of this survey, in particular its inclusion of several SBUs within the same parent corporation, requires careful interpretation and does not make it comparable to the previous one of large firms.

A recent survey of large organizations with multiple business units, divisional structures, a wide variety of product or service offerings, and wide geographic coverage found corporate structural change to be the ultimate driver of structural change in supply organizations (Johnson and Leenders, 2001). It did not find evidence that supply structures should be based on the advantages or disadvantages of centralized, hybrid, or decentralized structures. Indeed, as the authors noted (Johnson and Leenders, 2001, p. 11),

> It could be futile to change the supply organization structure without a corresponding change in the overall corporate structure. A more productive approach would bc to identify the opportunities for purchasing effectiveness and efficiency under the predetermined functional structure.

Commercial Examples

We will next review seven examples of how large commercial enterprises have organized their purchasing. For indirect goods and services, each of these corporations centralized supply strategy development, most at corporate headquarters. For direct goods and services, either individual SBUs developed supply strategies, or a lead SBU developed them for the entire enterprise.[5]

CAPS survey, for example, were two SBUs each from L-3 Communications, Lockheed Martin, Northrop Grumman, and Raytheon, and four SBUs from Boeing.

4 The reader may notice that the sum of aerospace and defense industry firms purchasing direct goods through *centralized*, *decentralized*, or *hybrid* organizations is 16, while 17 firms purchase indirect goods through such organizations. The discrepancy arises from one firm that purchases indirect goods from others but does not purchase direct goods (CAPS Research, 2005).

5 In fact, two of these corporations, Raytheon and Textron, faltered in their attempts to centralize supply strategy development for direct goods and services at corporate headquarters rather than with a lead SBU among their many diverse divisions.

Boeing

Boeing comprises SBUs and five subsidiaries. One of the SBUs is the Boeing Commercial Airplane Group (BCAG). The vice president and general manager of the Supply Management and Procurement Division, which is responsible for all component fabrication and purchasing, reports to an executive vice president of the business unit (Stundza, 2000). BCAG purchasing was reorganized when shortages of critical parts in the late 1990s prevented the company from meeting a surge of new orders. While retaining a base of nearly 3,000 suppliers, BCAG has also sought to consolidate purchasing efforts to maximize buying leverage. Other efforts included reducing the costs of purchased materials by at least 3 percent annually; reducing inventory, logistics, packaging, material handling, and related costs; initiating supplier "partnerships"; measuring the performance of suppliers, purchasing, and materials management; and initiating supplier training and buyer-supplier value-engineering projects. One example of a centralized system helping Boeing's decentralized operations is its replacement of more than 450 separate computer networks with four interconnected systems, giving 38,000 workers in eight states, Canada, and Australia a means of generating a single bill of materials for each component.

Another of Boeing's SBUs is the Shared Services Group (SSG), which is based in Bellevue, Washington, and has 21,000 employees. SSG provides the company's business units and world headquarters with a broad range of common services, including computing and network operations, e-business, facility services, employee benefits and programs, security, transportation, and the purchase of all nonproduction goods and services. The president of SSG reports to the office of the chairman. In integrating services, SSG has created "lean" processes and operations, leveraged buying power, and simplified access to services (Boeing Company, 2005a and 2005b). Among its achievements is a $1.4 billion reduction in infrastructure costs since 1998.

Hewlett-Packard

Following its merger with Compaq, HP developed a hybrid organization (Smock, 2005; Carbone, 2004). Before the merger, Compaq's centralized purchasing organization had strengths in aggregating requirements and leveraging purchases, while HP's more decentralized organization had experience involving buyers in new product development.

One impetus for the merger with Compaq was to achieve economy of scale in purchasing (Rudzki et al., 2006). As a result, after the merger, HP centralized purchasing for all commodities that all its businesses used but kept control of goods and services that were unique to the business within the business. For example, because motherboards are unique to different products—for example, desktop computers require different motherboards than do laptop (mobile) computers—purchasing for them remained decentralized.

Even for decentralized goods and services, HP leveraged its purchases through procurement councils that meet every month to discuss best practices, best processes, professional development, and information technology. The postmerger centralization efforts helped HP reduce the number of its direct material suppliers by half and its logistics providers by two-thirds from their premerger levels. Purchase of indirect goods and services was centralized at corporate headquarters in an indirect procurement organization, which was led by a vice president who reported to the executive vice president of global operations and information technology.

Recent restructuring eliminated HP's central purchasing organization, as well as many purchasing positions (Hannon, 2006). Under the restructuring, HP dissolved its Global Operations organization and moved its supply-chain, procurement, logistics, and order-fulfillment functions into its three business groups. The business groups were to have greater accountability over their operational activities, with one of them, the Personal Systems Group, hosting central direct procurement and carrying out procurement across the enterprise. Initial estimates indicated that the restructuring would eliminate 15,300 positions.

IBM

IBM's hardware business includes servers, storage, personal systems (recently sold to Lenovo), printing systems, and retail solutions. Other IBM businesses include software, services, financing, research, and technology (IBM Corporation, undated). In the early 1990s, IBM went through a major procurement transformation (Carbone, 1999). The company segmented its spending by commodity category and established 31 strategic commodity councils—18 for production, 13 for services and general support.[6]

The IBM procurement department sets the policies and guidelines for purchasing procedures for the corporation in a policy document called the "Blue Book." Annually, each council is required to develop a white paper specific to its commodity that details spend, market conditions, supplier segmentation, supply strategy, savings, etc.

Procurement at IBM is centralized but not necessarily at headquarters, particularly for production spending, with decentralized fulfillment. The head of the Production Commodity Council, who develops the centralized supply strategy jointly with representatives from the various businesses, is usually located where the bulk of product development and production takes place. Because there are often global requirements for a commodity, tactical buyers are required worldwide to fulfill orders in compliance with the centralized strategy.

The criteria IBM used for appointing and locating commodity councils included the locations of the best skills and best supplier relationships and where the goods and

---

[6] This section is largely based on a September 26, 2006, presentation on IBM's procurement transformation by Eric Niemann, Managing Consultant, Business Consulting Services, IBM Global Services, and subsequent e-mail exchanges.

services are developed. It is important for a production council to be involved early in the design process so that it can influence cost considerations throughout the engineering process. This was what typically drove the location of IBM's council personnel. Early involvement allows commodity councils to gain an adequate grasp of the technology roadmap and the direction of future technology so that they could share this information with key suppliers. The result was the creation of the best team of commodity buyers spread around the globe but managed centrally. The original central location tended to be where the bulk of the buy took place, but this has evolved over time.

The current vice president and chief procurement officer at IBM has recently relocated his office to Shenzhen, China, to get closer to suppliers (Carbone, 2006). Because IBM has outsourced a great deal of its manufacturing, the company's production footprint has also shifted. Likewise, the councils in some cases have had to adapt to these shifts and locate personnel in closer to the supplier(s) providing that production.

The services and general commodity council chairs responsible for the bulk of IBM's indirect spend are generally located in Somers (IBM headquarters), Endicott, and Poughkeepsie, New York, and in Raleigh, North Carolina. One council chair is in the United Kingdom, with other geographic representation elsewhere. Some IBM indirect spending is decentralized when there is a need for local diversity.

Lockheed Martin

Lockheed Martin works in five business areas: aeronautics, electronic systems, information and technology services, integrated systems and solutions, and space systems. Of its $35.5 billion in sales in 2004, 80 percent was to the U.S. government, 55 percent was to DoD, and 26 percent was to the Air Force.

The growth and changes the company was experiencing through acquisitions and divestitures, as well as the practices of the individual business units, meant the firm was not optimizing a total spend comprising about half its sales (Hannon, 2004). The firm therefore created its Corporate Shared Services organization to manage human resources; financial services; global supply-chain management (GSCM); and energy, environment, and health and safety management issues throughout the corporation. GSCM personnel are responsible for purchases involving more than one business unit, as well as supplier and subcontractor management.

Within the GSCM group, a strategic sourcing solutions group, with more than 50 employees led by a vice president, functions like an outside consultant to the business units and seeks to identify areas and suppliers to leverage enterprisewide help and to help negotiate improved "strategy-based" agreements. Lockheed Martin claims the group's efforts have yielded more than $200 million in savings in recent years.

One of the first efforts of the strategic sourcing solutions group was to identify an opportunity to reduce spend on machined parts, for which Lockheed Martin found it was spending at least 25 percent more than it should because of fragmentation.

A machining commodity council was formed, which reduced the supply base to preferred suppliers. When Lockheed Martin spending on integrated circuits was reduced significantly, the strategic sourcing solutions group worked with suppliers to ensure that pricing would not change. More generally, the strategic sourcing solutions group has sought to reduce prices from sole suppliers by using its leverage with those that also sell competitive goods and services to Lockheed Martin.

The strategic sourcing solutions group has recently shifted its focus from managing Lockheed Martin agreements with suppliers to managing the firm's relationships with suppliers (Avery, 2004). One recent effort it made to improve monitoring and supplier relationships was an agreement with a large computer hardware and software distributor. By working with the distributor, rather than separate OEMs, Lockheed Martin hopes to increase the leverage of its spend on information technology.

Raytheon

Raytheon comprises seven businesses: Integrated Defense Systems, Intelligence and Information Systems, Missile Systems, Network Centric Systems, Space and Airborne Systems, Raytheon Technical Services Company LLC, and Raytheon Aircraft Company. It has five enterprise supply-chain managers at the corporate level, including one for indirect material and one for direct material, who report to the vice president for enterprise supply-chain management and whose role is to organize supply-chain activities among diverse businesses across the company.

The company's enterprisewide supply-chain organization supports a wide diversity of manufacturing sites and is responsible for $8 billion in purchases annually, seeking to integrate and leverage goods and services requirements in the marketplace (Avery, 2001). Its initial centralization efforts met with some failures but improved when those for direct goods and services became more focused on the needs of the SBUs.

When initial efforts for purchasing centralization were resisted, Raytheon organized commodity teams to foster centralized processes with decentralized execution. Commodity teams were formed for semiconductors and passive electronic components, electromechanical hardware, interconnects, radio frequency and microwave, and machining and fabrication. Collectively, these teams have a $400 million spend. The commodity team leader is the supply-chain manager within the business responsible for the largest share of the spend. This "commodity expert" leads a team of peers who also have responsibility for buying the commodity. The team develops a written strategy using a supply-chain operations reference model, which is then introduced at the local level for execution.[7]

Raytheon has developed corporate agreements for some of its indirect spend, which totaled about $2.5 billion annually (Avery, 2001). Most material purchasing

---

[7] For more on supply-chain operations reference models, see Supply-Chain Council (2005). For more on Raytheon's supply base optimization efforts, see Gant et al. (2005).

is done by individual SBUs. Raytheon Aircraft Company has its own procurement group, which is a part of its Supply Chain Management Division and is responsible for purchasing the material, parts, and services required for production, nonproduction, and spares costs related to aircraft, aircraft spares, and aircraft services. In 2001, the Electronic Systems division (now part of Space and Airborne Systems) purchased most of the company's electronics (Hannon, 2001).

Textron

Textron is one of the country's largest multi-industry companies. Its 11 SBUs include Cessna Aircraft, Bell Helicopter, E-Z-GO, Jacobsen, Textron Fastening Systems, Greenlee, Textron Systems, Kautex, Textron Fluid & Power, Lycoming Engines, and Textron Financial. It works in ten different industries—aviation, defense, fastening, financial, fluid and power transmission, fuel systems, golf carts, industrial vehicles, tool, and turf care—in the United States and Europe.

Historically, buying at Textron has been highly decentralized, with major SBUs having the buying power (Avery, 2002). Typically, each business entered into its own agreements with key suppliers. Like those at Raytheon, efforts for consolidating purchases at Textron across the enterprise had limited success but improved when they became more focused on and incorporated more input from SBUs.

In 2000, the company formed a supply-chain council of procurement managers from key SBUs to determine what could be sourced collaboratively (Avery, 2002). Representatives from manufacturing and operations were subsequently added to the council. The supply-chain council did not centralize enterprise purchases, and management did not name a chief purchasing officer. Rather, the council is simply a vehicle for leveraging common purchases and sharing best practices across the businesses. A steering committee of SBU supply-chain executives selects commodities to be purchased, as well as the members of the teams that will purchase the commodities.

Commodity teams comprise representatives of businesses considered subject-matter experts and of related functions, such as finance and legal (Avery, 2002). Typically, the team leader represents a business that purchases a large volume of the commodity or who has expertise in the purchase.

One of the biggest opportunity areas Textron has pursued for centralization is the indirect goods and services that are used commonly throughout the company (Smock, 2003). Indirect product categories of goods and services include safety supplies, cylinder gases, chemicals, oils and lubricants, welding supplies, industrial supplies, contract labor, carbide inserts, office supplies, travel services, temporary labor, janitorial services, and maintenance of computer equipment. Efforts to centralize one of these commodities, cylinder gases, coincided and ultimately complemented the efforts of the supplier to develop more "strategic" accounts. The direct goods and services that Textron targeted for consolidated purchases included steel and plastic resins.

United Technologies

United Technologies Corporation (UTC) comprises seven large business units: Pratt and Whitney, Hamilton Sundstrand, Sikorsky, Otis Elevator, Carrier, UTC Fire and Security, and UTC Power. Each has multi–billion-dollar annual revenues and operates autonomously. Each also has its own separate supply management operation group supported by a corporate supply group for indirect purchases (Avery, 2006; Johnson, 2003).

Before UTC moved to consolidate its indirect purchasing, each business unit had acted independently of the others (Avery, 2003, 2006). By combining the indirect spend of business units, the company created $6 billion in annual purchasing volume, as well as enormous opportunities to leverage purchasing and consolidate the supply base. The centralized strategic sourcing operation and its cross-divisional, cross-functional commodity teams provided expertise and management that helped reduce costs for such items as human resources software by 70 percent, insurance actuarial services by 51 percent, engineering services by 45 percent, and demolition services by 19 percent. In 1998, UTC outsourced its procure-to-pay process to IBM, which provides the technology and initially helped with strategic sourcing. A recent Web-based crib-management system, used to distribute and track tools and other supplies and also functions as a front-end ordering and inventory-management system, helped reduce factory supply costs by 17 percent (Avery, 2005).

Procurement of direct materials remains with the business units in which it was consolidated. At Otis Elevator, for example, the vice president for supply management centralized some elements of purchasing, which had been a largely decentralized operation, with decentralized buyers using a centralized UTC model (Avery, 2000). In the first two years of the program, the production supplier base was more than halved; spend by long-term agreement increased sharply; and on-time delivery rates exceeded 90 percent.

UTC's three aerospace businesses—Hamilton Sunstrand, Pratt & Whitney, and Sikorsky—share many of the same suppliers, use similar parts families (Teague, 2006), and have been leveraging some of their spend for nearly 10 years. They jointly create corporate contracts with common terms and conditions, making it easier for suppliers to do business with UTC. The separate companies coordinate spending to leverage buying, which an aerospace subcommittee of the corporate Supply Management Council coordinates. The subcommittee includes the vice presidents of procurement for each aerospace division. Most of the leveraging is concentrated in about half the aerospace component families, such as bearings, fasteners, castings, forgings, fabrication, machined parts, and compressor airfoils. To enhance leverage, engineering works with a specific commodity manager, who lead teams of commodity representatives from each division. The commodity teams review their respective requirements and establish common engineering specifications and tolerances when possible so that they can use the same part or family of parts.

UTC's commercial businesses—Otis, Carrier, UTC Fire & Security, and UTC Power—have less opportunity to leverage their spending, with the exception of purchasing some metals, but their supply management operations frequently communicate with each other (Avery, 2006).

Automotive Supplier

One automotive supplier (Laseter, 1998) used the following process for determining where to develop different commodity strategies. It developed a standard commodity planning process to gain "expertise scale" through information sharing. Next it identified three possible models for managing different commodity groups:

1. centrally controlled and managed
2. managed by the lead division to ensure enterprisewide coverage with ownership by the business unit that is the key buyer
3. managed by each business unit according to a central process.

Each commodity group was then analyzed along six dimensions. Three of these—commonality of requirements, process modeling complexity, and corporate leverage—favor centralized, corporate control. Three others—business criticality, logistics integration, and design integration—favor business-unit control. Each commodity was given a high, medium, or low rating for each of the six categories, which determined the recommended responsibility model. The result was that some commodity groups were managed centrally, some were managed by the lead division, and some were managed by the business units.

Table B.4 summarizes how the firms reviewed above segment their supply strategies.

A Framework for Locating Centralized Supply Strategy Development Teams

If enterprises decide to centralize supply strategy development, where should they locate the multiskilled buying teams that will develop supply strategies and manage suppliers for various groups of related goods or services? We next consider this question further.

As noted in the main text, enterprises typically segment the goods and services they purchase according to their relative strategic value and vulnerability. They use very different strategies, tactics, technology, and personnel to acquire and manage them.[8]

---

[8] See Flynn and Farney (2000) for more on the different levels of education, technical knowledge, analytic capabilities, and experience required to develop and execute the different strategies and tactics needed to purchase goods and services in the different quadrants of the supply positioning matrix.

Table B.4
Commercial Examples of Supply Strategy Segmentation

Company	Indirect Spending (nonproduction)	Direct Spending (inputs to production)
Boeing	Centralized at headquarters	Centralized within SBUs Many joint strategies
HP	Centralized at one SBU[a]	Centralized at lead SBUs for common commodities
IBM	Primarily centralized at headquarters with geographic representatives	Centralized at SBU with the best skills, supplier relationships, and bulk of design and production
Lockheed Martin	Centralized at headquarters	Centralized within SBUs Few centralized at headquarters
Raytheon	Decentralized Few centralized at headquarters	Centralized within SBUs[b] Few centralized at lead SBU
Textron	Centralized at SBUs Few centralized at headquarters	Centralized within SBUs[b] Few centralized at lead SBU
United Technologies	Centralized at headquarters	Centralized within SBU

[a] Recently moved from headquarters to SBUs.

[b] Reportedly tried and failed to centralize direct spend at corporate headquarters.

While the development of an enterprise's supply strategies for the various groups of goods and services it purchases may be centralized, not all supply strategies may be developed within the same organization. That is, in many enterprises, purchases of indirect goods and services (goods and services that are not direct inputs to the enterprise's products or production processes), which are often of relatively low value and risk, are typically separate from purchases of higher value and higher risk direct goods and services (goods and services that are inputs to an enterprise's products or production processes), which require very different personnel skills, practices, processes, and systems. For example, as noted above, UTC has centralized purchases of indirect goods and services (information technology, human resources, marketing, travel, real estate, finance, and labor) at corporate headquarters, within an indirect procurement organization separate from direct spending for inputs to production.

For relatively small or very homogeneous enterprises (those in which all business units have the same mission, use the same inputs and suppliers, have the same production processes, produce the same outputs, and serve similar or the same customers), supply strategies and supplier relationships for most purchases are probably best developed where product design is located, at the enterprise's headquarters or in its largest business unit or facility, with execution either at the headquarters or delegated to local operations. This is because there is very little variability in each facility or business unit's strategic needs, customers, types and sizes of purchases, or technical and purchasing expertise or knowledge.

Global conglomerates (such as General Electric, UTC, Honeywell, Textron), on the other hand, have a particular challenge in deciding where to centralize supply strategy development and supplier management activities. These firms also offer a possible analogy for DoD and its constituent services and agencies. These enterprises have multiple, independently operated SBUs competing in different markets, each with different missions, requirements, organizational structures, cultures, processes, practices, inputs, and products that can vary substantially.[9] A conglomerate's business units are also likely to have different direct inputs, suppliers, and customers for their primary products and to share a number of common indirect purchases and suppliers. Even for direct purchases and suppliers, the strategic needs and size of purchases may vary considerably within a company.

One technique enterprises with multiple SBUs use to balance the need for common enterprisewide processes and the benefits of centralization against the desire to give individual SBUs full accountability for their operations and profitability is to establish different organizational structures for different types of purchases, developing a hybrid approach. This mixed approach to the alternatives of either centralizing to get more volume leverage or decentralizing to increase accountability and improve responsiveness to customers takes into account the specific characteristics of different types of purchased goods and services, as well as the unique requirements of the different SBUs for these goods and services (Eliff, 1998, especially pp. 44–45).

The following four criteria can be used to determine where to best locate the primary responsibility for developing a conglomerate's centralized supply strategy for each major commodity group of related goods and services that it purchases. These are:

1. strategic needs of the SBUs (e.g., mission criticality)
2. technical, industry, and purchasing expertise and knowledge
3. greatest industry leverage and strongest supplier relationships
4. commonality vice uniqueness across SBUs.

Strategic Needs of the SBUs

Each SBU's strategic needs for specific goods and services are determined by their value for its strategy, products, and customers and on the overall strategy of the enterprise. For example, if a specific good or service is critical to the competitive advantage (mission) of an SBU's product or the ability of the SBU to deliver that product, that good or service would be considered strategic to that SBU. A conglomerate may have other SBUs for which the same goods or services are less critical to products or customers or

---

9 Porter (1985) also notes that most major firms have divided their businesses into some type of SBUs and instituted formal planning processes in which SBUs submit plans for review by top management on an annual or biannual basis.

are not used at all. For example, in DoD, jet engines are critical to the ability of the Air Force to perform most of its missions. Other services also have weapon systems with jet or turbine engines, but they and their components are particularly strategic to the mission of the Air Force. When the strategic need for a particular good or service varies significantly among a conglomerate's SBUs, the one with the most strategic need for it should have the most responsibility and authority for developing the conglomerate's centralized supply strategy. If strategic need is broadly spread over each SBU and is very weak, as it can be for indirect goods and services, it may be best for the conglomerate's headquarters to have the most responsibility and authority for enterprisewide supply strategy development and supplier management.

Technical, Industry, and Purchasing Knowledge or Expertise

Because a conglomerate's SBUs typically have different products and compete in different industries or markets, their technical or engineering expertise for design, manufacturing, and product repair; their industry and supplier knowledge about key inputs to production; and, finally, the purchasing skills they require to acquire the inputs are all likely to vary. The SBU with the greatest technical or engineering expertise, industry knowledge, and purchasing skills for a specific commodity group is the most able to work with suppliers on commodity design and specification, craft a supply strategy, and manage productive supplier relationships. Thus, the development of supply strategy and management of suppliers is best done at the SBU with the strongest technical or engineering skills and the greatest knowledge of and expertise in purchasing in the industry. For example, because of the importance of jet engines to the Air Force, it has personnel who are technical experts in the design and repair of jet engines and their components, on the industry and suppliers that supply and repair them, and on the purchasing techniques used to acquire them. At the same time, the Army has technical experts on the design and repair of diesel-powered combustion engines and on the industry and suppliers and the typical purchasing practices used to acquire them. If no SBU in a conglomerate has superior technical, engineering, industry, or purchasing knowledge or expertise in a particular common commodity group, it would be best to develop the commodity group's supply strategy and management of suppliers at the conglomerate's headquarters.

Industry Leverage and Strength of Supplier Relationships

Industry leverage depends on an SBU's annual spend in the industry. The strength of the supplier relationship is based on the SBU's dollar volume with the supplier, as well as on the history and nature of past, current, and prospective business relations, particularly the contribution to supplier profitability. Thus, if one SBU in a conglomerate has a much higher spend in a particular industry or stronger relationships with key industry suppliers than other SBUs, it should probably be the lead developer and negotiator of the enterprise's centralized supply strategy for that industry and its suppliers.

The SBU's leverage would increase, and its supplier relationships would strengthen still further with control of enterprisewide spend, benefiting SBUs with a smaller spend and weaker supplier relationships.

A DoD example of this is the spend for wheeled vehicles. The Army has the largest spend and the longest and strongest supplier relationships in DoD for wheeled vehicles and the goods and services related to them. Thus, it makes sense for the Army, as an already concentrated center of spend, to be the home of a DoD wheeled-vehicle commodity team. The Marine Corps uses the same or very similar wheeled vehicles as the Army but has a much smaller spend for them. Thus, the Marine Corps may benefit from further leveraging the Army's spending and supplier relationships for wheeled vehicles.

RAND research on developing supply strategy for low-demand service parts provides additional commercial organizational examples for locating supply strategy development and supplier management based on leverage and supplier relationships. At a leading OEM known for working closely with key suppliers on product design and production, the business unit that purchases and manages inputs for production also purchases aftermarket service parts, even though a separate SBU is responsible for managing aftermarket support. These "production" contracts typically include provisions for service parts not only during production but also for a number of years after production has ended. This OEM strategically links and leverages purchase of aftermarket service parts to the purchase of production parts because the OEM has the most leverage with its suppliers when it selects sources for product production (equivalent to Air Force weapon system acquisition). The manufacturer claims that most suppliers prefer the steady, high-volume business of supplying production parts to the irregular, low-volume business of supplying service parts for the aftermarket (equivalent to Air Force sustainment parts). Product service and parts can have much higher margins than original equipment, which is why many OEMS seek to protect their postsale business. For example, commercial jet engines are often sold at break-even or even a loss, because such OEMs as General Electric view the sale of a jet engine as a "corporate annuity, a decades-long stream of very profitable parts and service sales" (Siekman, 2002). The OEM that RAND researchers investigated has representatives from its service parts business unit on its supply strategy development teams but places responsibility for managing the team and its suppliers with the business unit responsible for production. Performance evaluations for this OEM's suppliers include how they supplied both service parts and parts for production.

Commonality Versus Uniqueness Across SBUs

A conglomerate's SBUs are likely to purchase a mix of common and unique goods and services.

Indirect goods and services offer a good example of commonality. Most indirect goods and services are common across SBUs and are necessary for operations but are not directly linked to the strategic needs and operations of each SBU. These goods and services are typically supplied abundantly by highly competitive markets for which industry leverage and strength of supplier relationships are relatively weak and spread throughout SBUs. As a result, supply strategy development and supplier management for indirect goods and services are often centralized at an enterprise's headquarters, even in conglomerates with highly diverse and autonomous SBUs. In some enterprises, supply strategy development and supplier management for indirect commodities are consolidated in a separate SBU that reports directly to headquarters. Boeing is one example of this, as is the federal government's creation of GSA for purchasing common goods and services, such as office suppliers and building space, and DoD's creation of DLA to purchase common materials, such as food, clothing, medical suppliers, industrial hardware items, and fuel.

Some conglomerates have used a more voluntary approach to centralization of common SBU purchases at corporate headquarters. These conglomerates may establish a purchasing council for goods and services that multiple SBUs use that would benefit from a coordinated approach to suppliers and the supply market. Each SBU can choose to participate in the council when beneficial to do so, for instance, if the added value from pooling volume offset the need to agree to commonality and standardization across SBUs (Eliff, 1998).

For goods and services that add relatively low value and for which there is little volume leverage to be gained from centralizing purchasing (that is, for low-value support items that add little functional value), a user-direct approach may work best. This approach seeks to minimize purchase transaction costs by using simplified methods, such as using a purchase card for charging and billing expenditures. Some who have done this, however, have seen their leverage decrease and have subsequently created centralized agreements and Web pages through which users now make the vast bulk of their card purchases.

Unique or less-common SBU purchases are most often for direct materials, which tend to be more complex and challenging to purchase and manage. Supply strategy development and supplier relationships for goods and services that are unique to an SBU or that represent a significant share of the SBU's total cost structure are typically located at that SBU. Supply strategy development and supplier management for goods and services that are common or critical to a few, but not all, SBUs are typically located at the SBU with the most strategic need and leverage, greatest technical knowledge, strongest supplier relationships, and the most technical and purchasing expertise.

Even though the authority and responsibility for the development of supply strategies and supplier relationships within a conglomerate may be centrally located at one SBU, representatives from other SBUs that also purchase the good or service also participate in the strategy development teams to make sure that their requirements are properly considered and included in strategy development and supplier management.

Actual purchases off centralized agreements are typically centralized to the SBU with the specific requirement.

APPENDIX C

Prospective Supply Risks

Several sources outline prospective risks that enterprises must address in devising supply strategies (see Chapter Five, particularly text on step 11). The information we present below is a composite of material drawn from Peck et al. (2003), Ziegengein and Nienhaus (2004), and Steele and Court (1996).

External

The **external** risks an enterprise may face fall into the categories of *demand, supply, technology, good or service,* and *environment.* The following subsections treat each of these in turn.

Demand Uncertainty

Demand uncertainty is the simplest category, consisting of *surges* and *shortfalls.*

Supply

Supply is the most complex, encompassing such areas as the balance between supply and demand, the availablity and cost of raw materials, market complexities, the natures of suppliers, and shipping issues.

The issues related to the **balance between supply and demand** include the percentage of the market and the percentage of the supplier's production the buyer requires, the demands of other buyers, the risk of shortages, the overall volumes of raw materials, and how future requirements compare with future availability.

An additional concern about **raw materials** are their availability to the *supplier*:

- location, certainty of supplier continuation, etc.
- the nature of the materials
- the source
- the potential for supply disruption (as, perhaps, a result of local political or regional instability)
- the risk of natural disasters.

Cost trends for raw materials are also a factor. The price outlook is one factor, and another is the existence of events or developments that are likely to trigger substantial price increases.

The **overall market** may be complicated by the existence of cartels, the relative strengths of the buyers and sellers in the market, and restraints on others entering the market.

Beyond the basic availability of materials and their cost, **suppliers** themselves present certain risks:

- finance
  - trends in profitability
  - cash flow
  - availability of parent-company guarantees
  - bankruptcy and/or financial failure
- marketplace behavior
  - pricing policy pursued
  - price trends compared to inflation
  - willingness to discount
  - price compared to competitors
  - share of market
  - influencer or follower
  - extent of any monopoly
- management attitude
  - extent of openness and trust
  - willingness to continually change and improve
- withdrawal from the market
- inability to sustain during a downturn
  - utilize slack
  - reserve funds
- inadequate contingency and risk management planning
- poor quality, rework
  - failure to maintain equipment
  - lack of training in principles and techniques
- constrained volume capacity
  - equipment, personnel, or facilities
- inflexible mix (i.e., production) capability
- shortage of inputs (materials and services)
  - poor forecasting
  - long and/or variable purchasing cycle times
- long lead or order cycle times—unresponsive
  - backlogs

- variable lead or order cycle times—unreliable
- inability to control or reduce costs
- unwillingness or inability to continually improve
- high management and/or personnel turnover
- slow adoption of technological changes
- incompatible information systems
- dependency on buyer, one, or a few large customers
- production, shipping, and distribution methods
  - production method (safety and environmental implications, batch or continuous flow, retooling time, economic minimum quantities)
  - production location(s) (flexibility to manufacture at other sites)
  - distribution (special handling or storage problems, special packaging problems).

Shipping is a final supply concern. Constraints, for example, may include the availability of such *infrastructure* as ports, roads, railroads, and airports); such *assets* as cargo aircraft, container ships, locomotives and rail cars, chassies, and containers; and such *labor* as truck drivers, rail operators, longshoremen, and pilots. The need to travel *long distances* can increase lead times, the chance of disruption, and the chance of damage in transit. The many possible *touch points* raise further concerns about security, theft, terrorism, tampering, and damage and may increase costs—and various stages of transit may have incompatible information technologies.

Technological Risk

The elements of **technological uncertainty** are the overall availability, obsolescence, the pace of change, direction of change, and the rate of technical innovation (and its effects on availability and obsolescence). Questions that affect rate of innovation are the frequency of new ideas or concepts, product life cycles, and emerging technologies.

Type of Good or Service

The *type of good or service* an enterprise is offering may also be in question. What is the *design*? Is the product *manufacturable*? What is its *value* to the enterprise (in terms of its effects on customer satisfaction and loyalty, liability, and costs and profits)? What *value* does it add to the *final product or application* (in terms of customer demand, uniqueness, substitutability, system integration)?

Environmental

Enterprises function in the midst of both the human, social, and political world and the natural world.

Natural Disasters. Among these are such *weather phenomena* as hurricanes, cyclones, tornados, rogue waves, blizzards, hailstorms, lightning, floods, mudslides, and droughts; such *geological phenomena* as volcanoes, earthquakes, and tsunamis; and such *biological phenomena* as epidemics and infestations.

Human Activity. People can also damage property or impede business. This may occur by accident, through a fire, explosions structural failure, or hazardous spill. But it can also be deliberate, and the possibilities include *terrorism or sabotage,* such as bombings, a chemical or biological release, blockades, product tampering, or an electronic intrusion (viruses, worms, trojan horses, denial of service attacks). Physical and intellectual property may be *stolen.* Finally, *acts of war* may include bombings and blockades.

Market Environment. Within a given market, prices may be unstable and currency rates uncertain. There may be capacity constraints, yet little or no competition because of such entry barriers as requirements for capital and other specific assets, lack of access to such proprietary information as patents, and concerns about designs and processes. Potential producers may see the item as having low profitability or may be concerned about certification and qualification demands. Producers may also be concerned about the availability of and cost trends for raw materials and the geographic concentration of suppliers.

Business Environment. Additional facts of life that influence the business environment include government actions, such as taxes, tariffs, regulations, customs, and currency devaluations; economic recessions or depressions; labor issues, including shortages and unrest (such as strikes and work slowdowns); political unrest or instability, perhaps boycotts; and fear of lawsuits over environmental, health and safety, or intellectual-property matters.

Internal

Enterprises also face **internal** risks. For example, a company may have inadequate controls on its internal supply chain, perhaps due to failures in inventory management, demand forecasting, and manufacturing scheduling. It may have problems with processes or its plant. The company might even have issues with its contingency planning and mitigation, perhaps lacking an adequate risk management program identifying risks and options.

Bibliography

A. T. Kearney, Inc., "Creating Value Through Strategic Supply Management: Assessment of Excellence in Procurement," Chicago, 2004. As of September 14, 2006:
http://www.atkearney.com/shared_res/pdf/AEP_2004_S.pdf

Aberdeen Group, Inc., "Spend Visibility: Maximizing Value in Strategic Sourcing," executive white paper, Boston, August 2002.

Anderson, Erin, and Sandy D. Jap, "The Dark Side of Close Relationships," *MIT Sloan Management Review*, Vol. 46, No. 3, Spring 2005, pp. 75–82.

Artman, Les, and Joe Martha, "Establishing Long Term Relationships," *Transportation and Distribution*, Vol. 38, No. 3, March 1997, pp. 69–72.

Avery, Susan, "Supply Chain Management at Otis Reins in Global Spending," *Purchasing*, June 1, 2000. As of July 8, 2005:
http://www.purchasing.com/article/CA138834.html

———, "Linking Supply Chains Saves Raytheon $400 Million," *Purchasing*, August 23, 2001. As of July 8, 2005:
http://www.purchasing.com/article/CA152189.html

———, "Transforming Textron," *Purchasing*, October 10, 2002. As of July 8, 2005:
http://www.purchasing.com/article/CA250886.html

———, "Purchasing Turns to Services to Keep Cost Savings Coming," *Purchasing*, October 9, 2003. As of July 8, 2005:
http://www.purchasing.com/article/CA327463.html

———, "How Suppliers Measure Up for Lockheed Martin," *Purchasing*, February 19, 2004. As of November 10, 2005:
http://www.purchasing.com/article/CA381820.html

———, "Factory Supplies Team Kicks It Up a Notch," *Purchasing*, October 6, 2005. As of December 1, 2005:
http://www.purchasing.com/article/CA6261052.html

———, "Supply Management Is Core of Success at UTC," *Purchasing*, September 7, 2006. As of September 30, 2006:
http://www.purchasing.com/article/CA6368274.html

B. F. Goodrich Aerospace, presentation to Air Education and Training Command Strategic Outsourcing Seminar, Randolph Air Force Base, Tex., October 16, 1997.

Baily, Peter, David Farmer, David Jessop, and David Jones, *Purchasing Principles and Management*, 9th ed., Harlow, England: Prentice Hall, 2005.

Baldwin, Laura H., Frank Camm, and Nancy Y. Moore, *Federal Contract Bundling: A Framework for Making and Justifying Decisions for Purchased Services*, Santa Monica, Calif.: RAND Corporation, MR-1224-AF, 2001. As of May 16, 2005:
http://www.rand.org/pubs/monograph_reports/MR1224/

Bradley, Peter, "Triple Play!" *Logistics Management*, February 1997.

Boeing Company, "Boeing Shared Services: Overview," 2005a. As of July 6, 2005:
http://www.boeing.com/ssg/ssg-backgrounder.html

———, "Boeing Overview," February 2005b. As of July 6, 2005:
http://www.boeing.com/companyoffices/aboutus/brief.html

Bowersox, John J., David J. Closs, and M. Bixby Cooper, *Supply Chain Logistics Management*, New York: McGraw-Hill, 2002.

Burt, David N., and Richard L. Pinkerton, *A Purchasing Manager's Guide to Strategic Proactive Procurement*, New York: American Management Association, 1996.

Business Wire, "World-Class Procurement Spends 27 Percent More on Technology While Dramatically Cutting Overall Costs," February 15, 2005.

CAPS Research, "Defining the Procurement Organization—2004," Tempe, Ariz., June 2, 2004.

———, "Purchasing Performance Benchmarking Report for the Aerospace/Defense Industry," Tempe, Ariz., January 24, 2005.

Carbone, James, "Reinventing Purchasing Wins the Medal for Big Blue," *Purchasing*, September 16, 1999. As of September 30, 2006:
http://www.purchasing.com/article/CA147393.html

———, "Motorola Simplifies to Lower Costs," *Purchasing*, October 18, 2001. As of October 2, 2006:
http://www.purchasing.com/article/CA170584.html

———, "Hewlett-Packard Wins for the 2nd Time," *Purchasing*, September 2, 2004. As of July 7, 2005:
http://www.purchasing.com/article/CA451858.html

———, "IBM to Move Purchasing Headquarters to China," *Purchasing*, May 25, 2006. As of October 2, 2006:
http://www.purchasing.com/article/CA6338223.html

Carter, Joseph, "Development of Supply Strategies," in Joseph L. Cavinato and Ralph G. Kauffmann, eds., *The Purchasing Handbook: A Guide for the Purchasing and Supply Professional*, New York: McGraw-Hill, 1999, pp. 81–98.

Christie, Rebecca, "Pentagon Under Pressure to Explain Report of $20 Ice Tray," *Wall Street Journal*, November 2, 2005.

Christopher, Martin, *Understanding Supply Chain Risk: A Self-Assessment Workbook*, Cranfield, United Kingdom: Cranfield School of Management, 2003. As of November 12, 2006:
http://www.som.cranfield.ac.uk/som/research/centres/lscm/downloads/60599WOR.PDF

Cox, Andrew, "Understanding Buyer and Supplier Power: A Framework for Procurement and Supply Competence," *The Journal of Supply Chain Management*, Vol. 37, No. 2, Spring 2001, pp. 8–15.

Coyle, John J., Edward J. Bardi, and C. John Langley Jr., *The Management of Business Logistics: A Supply Chain Perspective*, Mason, Ohio: South-Western/Thomson Learning, 2003.

Crawford, Gordon, *Variability in the Demands for Aircraft Spare Parts: Its Magnitude and Implications*, Santa Monica, Calif.: RAND Corporation, R-3318-AF, 1988. As of June 12, 2007: http://www.rand.org/pubs/reports/R3318/

Day, George S., *Analysis for Strategic Market Decisions*, St. Paul, Minn.: West Publishing Company, 1986.

Derkinderen, Frans G. J., and Roy L. Crum, "Pitfalls in Using Portfolio Techniques—Assessing Risk and Potential," *Long Range Planning*, Vol. 17, No. 2, April 1984, pp. 129–136.

Dixon, Lloyd, Chad Shirley, Laura H. Baldwin, John A. Ausink, and Nancy Campbell, *An Assessment of Air Force Data on Contract Expenditures*, Santa Monica, Calif.: RAND Corporation, MR-274-AF, 2005. As of December 7, 2005: http://www.rand.org/pubs/monographs/MG274/

Dobler, Donald W., and David N. Burt, *Purchasing and Supply Management: Text and Cases*, 6th ed., New York: McGraw-Hill, 1996.

DoD—See U.S. Department of Defense.

Dolan, Tim, and Karen M. Fedele, "Strategic Sourcing: Reducing Cost and Supporting Diversity Goals," presented to the Institute for Supply Management, 89th Annual International Supply Management Conference, Philadelphia, April 2004.

Dubois, Anna, and Ann-Charlott Pedersen, "Why Relationships Do Not Fit into Purchasing Portfolio Models—A Comparison Between the Portfolio and Industrial Network Approaches," *European Journal of Purchasing and Supply Management*, Vol. 8, No. 1, March 2002, pp. 35–42.

Duffy, Roberta, "Supply Base Rationalization," Center for Advanced Purchasing Studies, Critical Issues Report, January 2005. As of May 16, 2005: http://www.capsresearch.org/publications/pdfs-protected/cir012005.pdf

Dyer, Jeffrey H., Dong Sung Cho, and Wujin Chu, "Strategic Supplier Segmentation: The Next 'Best Practice' in Supply Chain Management," *California Management Review*, Vol. 40, No. 2, Winter 1998, pp. 57–77.

Eliff, Scott A., "Organizing for Excellence: Five Case Studies," *Supply Chain Management Review*, Vol. 1, No. 4, Winter 1998, pp. 38–45.

Ellram, Lisa M., *Strategic Cost Management in the Supply Chain: A Purchasing and Supply Management Perspective*, Tempe, Ariz.: CAPS Research, August 2002.

Ellram, Lisa M., and Thomas Choi, *Supply Management for Value Enhancement*, Tempe, Ariz.: National Association of Purchasing Management, 2000.

Ellram, Lisa M., and Sue P. Siferd, "Total Cost of Ownership: A Key Concept in Strategic Cost Management Decisions," *Journal of Business Logistics*, Vol. 19, No. 1, 1998, pp. 55–84.

Ellison, Sarah, Ann Zimmerman, and Charles Forelle, "P&G's Gillette Edge: The Playbook It Honed at Wal-Mart," *Wall Street Journal*, January 31, 2005.

Eversbusch, Andreas W., "Achieving Breakthrough Results Through Strategic Sourcing," presented at Strategic Sourcing Management Conference, Institute for International Research, New Orleans, February 1998.

Fawcett, Stanley E., *The Supply Management Environment*, Tempe, Ariz.: Institute for Supply Management, 2000.

Flynn, Anna E., and Sam Farney, *The Supply Management Leadership Process*, Tempe, Ariz.: National Association of Purchasing Management, 2000.

Gant, Karen, Dawn Garrett, Linda Keenan, Kelly O'Dell, and Shirley Patterson, "A Case Study: Raytheon Supply Base Optimization Project," presentation to the National Contract Management Association World Congress, Phoenix, Ariz., April 2005. As of December 2, 2005: http://www.ncmahq.org/presentations/wc05/Supply_Chain_Management/708_Reeds.ppt

Gelderman, Cees J., and Arjan J. van Weele, "Strategic Direction Through Purchasing Portfolio Management: A Case Study," *The Journal of Supply Chain Management*, Vol. 38, No. 2, Spring 2002, pp. 30–37.

———, "Purchasing Portfolio Models: A Critique and Update," *Journal of Supply Chain Management*, Vol. 41, No. 3, Summer 2005, pp. 19–28.

Gerstner, Louis V., Jr., *Who Says Elephants Can't Dance? Inside IBM's Historic Turnaround*, New York: HarperBusiness, 2002.

Giunipero, Larry E., and Reham Aly Eltantawy, "Securing the Upstream Supply Chain: A Risk Management Approach," *International Journal of Physical Distribution and Logistics Management*, Vol. 34, No. 9, 2004, pp. 698–713.

Goldfeld, Charles, *Supplier Strategies*, West Palm Beach, Fla.: PT Publications, 1999.

Hahn, Chan K., Hyoo H. Kim, and Iong S. Kim, "Costs of Competition: Implications for Purchasing Strategy," *Journal of Purchasing and Materials Management*, Vol. 22, No. 3, Fall 1986, pp. 2–7.

Hammer, Michael, *Beyond Reengineering: How the Process-Centered Organization Is Changing Our Work and Our Lives*, New York: HarperBusiness, 1996.

Hannon, Dave, "HP Realignment Impacts Purchasing and Supply Chain Operations," *Purchasing*, June 27, 2006. As of September 21, 2006: http://www.purchasing.com/article/CA6347612.html

———, "Raytheon Moves Ahead in Electronics Buying," *Purchasing*, August 23, 2001. As of July 8, 2005: http://www.purchasing.com/article/CA152188.html

———,"Lockheed Martin: Negotiators Inc.," *Purchasing*, February 5, 2004. As of December 19, 2005: http://www.purchasing.com/article/CA378931.html

Hicks, Donald A., "The State of Supply Chain Strategy," in John Woods, ed., *The Purchasing and Supply Handbook*, Tempe, Ariz.: National Association of Purchasing Management, 2000.

Hirsch, Chet, and Marcos Barbalho, "Toward World-Class Procurement," *Supply Chain Management Review*, Vol. 5, No. 6, November–December 2001, pp. 74–80.

IBM Corporation, "About IBM," Web page, Armonk, N.Y., undated. As of November 20, 2006: http://www.ibm.com/ibm/us/

John Deere and Company, "Sourcing Strategies," Deere & Company Supply Management, 1997.

Johnson, Clay, III, Deputy Director for Management, Office of Management and Budget, "Implementing Strategic Sourcing," memorandum for chief acquisition officers, chief financial officers, and chief information officers, May 20, 2005. As of June 13, 2005: http://www.whitehouse.gov/omb/procurement/comp_src/implementing_strategic_sourcing.pdf

Johnson, P. Fraser, "Supply Organizational Structures," *Critical Issues Report*, August 2003. As of July 8, 2005:
http://www.capsresearch.org/Publications/pdfs-protected/cir082003.pdf

Johnson, P. Fraser, and Michiel R. Leenders, "The Supply Organizational Structure Dilemma," *Journal of Supply Chain Management*, Vol. 37, No. 3, Summer 2001, pp. 4–11.

———, *Supply's Organizational Roles and Responsibilities*, Tempe, Ariz.: CAPS Research, 2004.

Joint Chiefs of Staff, *Joint Vision 2020*, Washington, D.C., 2000. As of June 13, 2005:
http://www.dtic.mil/jointvision/jvpub2.htm

Kaufman, Allen, Craig H. Wood, and Gregory Theyel, "Collaboration and Technology Linkages: A Strategic Supplier Typology," *Strategic Management Journal*, Vol. 21, No. 6, June 2000, pp. 649–663.

Kiser, James, and George Cantrell, "6 Steps to Managing Risk," *Supply Chain Management Review*, Vol. 10, No. 3, April 2006, pp. 12–17.

Kraljic, Peter, "Purchasing Must Become Supply Management," *Harvard Business Review*, Vol. 61, No. 5, September 1983, pp. 109–117.

Laseter, Timothy M., *Balanced Sourcing: Cooperation and Competition in Supplier Relationships*, San Francisco: Jossey-Bass Publishers, 1998.

Leenders, Michiel R., Harold E. Fearon, Anna E. Flynn, and P. Fraser Johnson, *Purchasing and Supply Management*, 12th ed., New York: McGraw-Hill Irwin, 2002.

Linstone, Harold A., and Murray Turoff, eds., *The Delphi Method: Techniques and Applications*, 2002. As of October 3, 2006:
http://www.is.njit.edu/pubs/delphibook/delphibook.pdf

Mariotti, John, "The Trust Factor in Supply Chain Management," *Supply Chain Management Review*, Vol. 3, No. 1, Spring 1999, pp. 70–77.

Markowitz, Harry, "Portfolio Selection," *The Journal of Finance*, Vol. 7, No. 1, March 1952, pp. 71–91.

Monczka, Robert M., Robert J. Trent, and Robert B. Handfield, *Purchasing and Supply Chain Management*, 2nd ed., Cincinnati, Ohio: South-Western College Pub., 2002.

Moore, Nancy Y., Laura H. Baldwin, Frank Camm, and Cynthia R. Cook, *Implementing Best Purchasing and Supply Management Practices: Lessons from Innovative Commercial Firms*, Santa Monica, Calif.: RAND Corporation, DB-334-AF, 2002. As of January 26, 2005:
http://www.rand.org/pubs/documented_briefings/DB334/

Moore, Nancy Y., Cynthia Cook, Clifford Grammich, and Charles Lindenblatt, *Using a Spend Analysis to Help Identify Prospective Air Force Purchasing and Supply Management Initiatives: Summary of Selected Findings*, Santa Monica, Calif.: RAND Corporation, DB-434-AF, April 2004. As of January 13, 2005:
http://www.rand.org/pubs/documented_briefings/DB434

Moore, Nancy Y., Clifford A. Grammich, Mary E. Chenoweth, and Judith D. Mele, *Targets for Marine Corps Purchasing and Supply Management Initiatives: Spend Analysis Findings*, Santa Monica, Calif.: RAND Corporation, DB-512-USMC, forthcoming.

Motley, Robert, "Nike's European 'Hot Banana,'" *American Shipper*, September 1995.

Nelson, Dave, Rick Mayo, and Patricia E. Moody, *Powered by Honda: Developing Excellence in the Global Enterprise*, New York: John Wiley and Sons, 1998.

Nelson, Dave, Patricia E. Moody, and Jonathan Stegner, *The Purchasing Machine: How the Top Ten Companies Use Best Practices to Manage Their Supply Chains*, New York: Free Press, 2001.

Nicosia, Nancy, and Nancy Y. Moore, *Implementing Purchasing and Supply Chain Management: Best Practices in Market Research*, Santa Monica, Calif.: RAND Corporation, MG-473-AF, 2006. As of March 27, 2007:
http://www.rand.org/pubs/monographs/MG473/

Niemann, Eric, Managing Consultant, Business Consulting Services, IBM, presentation on IBM's procurement transformation September 26, 2006.

O'Conner, Brian J., "Developing Procurement Strategies for Successful Supply Chain Management Operations," *Proceedings of the Fifth Annual Performance Measurement for the Purchasing Function Conference*, Boston, Mass.: Institute of International Research, June 2000.

Olsen, Rasmus Friis, and Lisa M. Ellram, "A Portfolio Approach to Supplier Relationships," *Industrial Marketing Management*, Vol. 26, No. 2, March 1997, pp. 101–113.

Ouellette, Ron, and Jay Pettinger, "Microsoft Manages Growth with an Integrated Facilities Management Agreement," presentation to Tradeline New Facility Management Strategies conference, San Diego, August 1997.

Owens, Gregory, Oliver Vidal, Rick Toole, and Donovan Favre, "Strategic Sourcing: Aligning Procurement Needs with Your Business Goals," in John Gattorna, ed., *Strategic Supply Chain Alignment: Best Practices in Supply Chain Management*, Gower, England: Andersen Consulting, 1998, pp. 285–301.

Peck, Helen, Jennifer Abley, Martin Christopher, Marc Haywood, Richard Waw, Christine Rutherford, and Mark Strathern, *Creating Resilient Supply Chains: A Practical Guide*, Cranfield, U.K.: Cranfield University, School of Management, Department for Transport, 2003. As of September 22, 2006:
http://www.som.cranfield.ac.uk/som/research/centres/lscm/downloads/57081_Report_AW.pdf

Pinkham, Paul, "Bogus Military Suppliers Sentenced," *Florida Times-Union*, July 6, 2005.

Porter, Anne Millen, "Spend a Little, Save a Lot!" *Purchasing*, April 4, 2002. As of July 5, 2005:
http://www.purchasing.com/article/CA203228.html

———, "Containing Total Spend," *Purchasing*, November 6, 2003. As of July 5, 2005:
http://www.purchasing.com/article/CA337312.html

Porter, Michael E., "Note on the Structural Analysis of Industries," Harvard Business School Note 376-054, Boston, Mass.: Harvard Business School Publishing, 1975.

———, *Competitive Strategy*, New York: Free Press, 1980.

———, *Competitive Advantage: Creating and Sustaining Superior Performance*, New York: Free Press, 1985.

Raedels, Alan R., *The Supply Management Process*, Tempe, Ariz.: Institute for Supply Management, 2000.

Riggs, David A., and Sharon L. Robbins, *The Executive's Guide to Supply Management Strategies: Building Supply Chain Thinking into All Business Processes*, New York: AMACOM, 1998.

Roberts, Julia S., "Help Wanted: Business and Supply Management," *Inside Supply Management*, December 2002.

Rudzki, Robert A., Douglas A. Smock, Michael Katzorke, and Shelley Stewart, Jr., *Straight to the Bottom Line: An Executive's Roadmap to World Class Supply Management*, Fort Lauderdale, Fla.: J. Ross Publishing, 2006.

Savoie, Major Scott, "Data Visibility—Problems and Solutions," PSCM Training—Strategic Sourcing, briefing, Hill Air Force Base, March 5, 2003.

Sawchuk, Chris, "Determining How to Measure the Success of Your Strategic Sourcing Initiative to Highlight Areas for Improvement," Institute for International Research Strategic Sourcing Contest, Chicago, June 2002.

Schellhorn, Gerhard, Andreas Thums, and Wolfgang Reif, "Formal Fault Tree Semantics," *Integrated Design and Process Technology*, June 2002, p. 1.

Sheffi, Yosef, *The Resilient Enterprise: Overcoming Vulnerability for Competitive Advantage*, Cambridge, Mass.: MIT Press, 2005.

Sheffi, Yosef, and James B. Rice, Jr., "A Supply Chain View of the Resilient Enterprise," *MIT Sloan Management Review*, Vol. 47, No. 1, Fall 2005, pp. 41–48.

Siekman, Philip, "GE Bets Big on Jet Engines," *Fortune*, December 19, 2002. As of October 4, 2007: http://money.cnn.com/magazines/fortune/fortune_archive/2002/12/30/334574/index.htm

Smeltzer, Larry R., and Joseph R. Carter, "How to Build an E-Procurement Strategy," *Supply Chain Management Review*, Vol. 5, No. 2, March 2001, pp. 76–83.

Smock, Doug, "Partnering Pays Off," *Purchasing*, September 4, 2003. As of March 27 2007: http://www.purchasing.com/article/CA319621.html

———, "Strategic Sourcing: It's Now Deeply Rooted in U.S. Buying," *Purchasing*, September 2, 2004. As of October 4, 2007:
http://www.purchasing.com/article/CA451867.html

———, "Hewlett-Packard: What's New," GlobalCPO.com, 2005. As of July 6, 2005:
http://globalcpo.com/_wsn/page6.html

Steele, Paul, and Brian H. Court, *Profitable Purchasing Strategies: A Manager's Guide for Improving Organizational Competitiveness Through the Skills of Purchasing*, London: McGraw-Hill Book Co., 1996.

Stephens, Dave, "Why Center-Led Procurement Is Gaining Purchasing Popularity," *Purchasing*, February 3, 2005. As of October 4, 2007:
http://www.purchasing.com/article/CA502341.html

Stundza, Tom, "New Era Dawns at Boeing," *Purchasing*, August 10, 2000. As of December 19, 2005: http://www.purchasing.com/index.asp?layout=articleWebzine&articleid=CA139404&

Supply-Chain Council, Supply-Chain Operations Reference Model: Overview Version 7.0, Washington, D.C., 2005. As of July 8, 2005:
http://www.supply-chain.org/page.ww?section=SCOR+Model&name=SCOR+Model

Syson, Russell, *Improving Purchase Performance*, London: Pitman, 1992.

Tang, Christopher S., "Supplier Relationship Map," *International Journal of Logistics: Research and Applications*, Vol. 2, No. 1, July 1999, pp. 39–56.

Teague, Paul E., "Cross-Divisional Teamwork Nets Big Savings," *Purchasing*, September 7, 2006. As of October 2, 2006:
http://www.purchasing.com/article/CA6368273.html

Trent, Robert J., "Applying TQM to SCM," *Supply Chain Management Review*, May–June 2001, pp. 70–78.

Turnbull, Peter W., "A Review of Portfolio Planning Models for Industrial Marketing and Purchasing Management," *European Journal of Marketing*, Vol. 24, No. 3, March 1990, pp. 7–22.

U.S. Air Force, Directorate of Innovation and Transformation, "Future Financials: More Combat Capability for the Dollar Spent," executive white paper, September 2004.

U.S. Air Force, Future Concepts and Transformation Division, *The U.S. Air Force Transformation Flight Plan*, November 2003. As of June 13, 2005:
http://www.af.mil/library/posture/AF_TRANS_FLIGHT_PLAN-2003.pdf

U.S. Department of Defense, "Transformation Planning Guidance," Washington, D.C., April 2003. As of February 15, 2005:
http://www.defenselink.mil/brac/docs/transformationplanningapr03.pdf

———, "DoD-Wide Strategic Sourcing Program: Concept of Operations," Washington, D.C., January 14, 2005.

U.S. Senate Committee on Armed Services, *Report on National Defense Authorization Act for Fiscal Year 2006*, Washington, D.C., May 17, 2005. As of June 13, 2005:
http://frwebgate.access.gpo.gov/cgi-bin/getdoc.cgi?dbname=109_cong_reports&docid=f:sr069.109.pdf

Van De Ven, Andrew H., and André L. Delbecq, "The Effectiveness of Nominal, Delphi, and Interacting Group Decision Making Processes," *Academy of Management Journal*, Vol. 17, No. 4, December 1974, pp. 605–621.

Van Weele, Arjan J., *Purchasing Management: Analysis, Planning and Practice*, London: Chapman and Hall, 1995.

White, Michael, "Establishing Competitive Advantage Through Significant Capital and Operational Cost Reductions," presented at INTERLOG 2002: The Aftermarket and Service Parts Logistics Conference, San Diego, June 2002.

Williams, Charlie E., Jr., "The Five Principles of Commodity Councils," *AQC On Point*, June 6, 2005. As of June 18, 2005:
https://www.safaq.hq.af.mil/contracting/aqccorner/pdf/onpoint-06jun05.pdf

Williamson, Oliver E., *The Economic Institutions of Capitalism*, New York: Free Press, 1985.

Ziegengein, Arne, and Jörg Niehnaus, "Coping with Supply Chain Risks on Strategic, Tactical, and Operational Levels," *Global Project and Manufacturing Management*, Symposium Proceedings, May 2004.

Zsidisin, George A., Alex Panelli, and Rebecca Upton, "Purchasing Organization Involvement in Risk Assessments, Contingency Plans, and Risk Management: An Exploratory Study," *Supply Chain Management*, Vol. 5, No. 4, 2000.

Zsidisin, George A., Gary L. Ragatz, and Steven A. Melnyk, "Effective Practices in Business Continuity Planning for Purchasing and Supply Management," *Department of Marketing and Supply Chain Management*, East Lansing, Mich.: Michigan State University, Eli Broad Graduate School of Management, July 21, 2003. As of September 22, 2006:
http://www.bus.msu.edu/msc/documents/AT&T%20full%20paper.pdf

———, "The Dark Side of Supply Chain Management," *Supply Chain Management Review*, Vol. 9, No. 2, March 2005, pp. 46–52.